SIMPLY FRENCH
IN AMERICA

SIMPLY FRENCH IN AMERICA

Homemade Family Meals and More

By: Sandrine Pilaz

This work is part memoir and includes events and conversations based upon the author's memory and conversations with several friends and family members. Some names and identifying details have been changed to protect the privacy of certain individuals and businesses.

The information contained in this book has been compiled from sources deemed reliable and it is accurate to the best of the author's knowledge; however, the author cannot guarantee its accuracy and validity and cannot be held liable for any errors or omissions.

Simply French in America: Homemade Family Meals and More
Copyright © 2022 by Sandrine Pilaz. All right reserved.

Book Cover and illustrations designed by Vincent Négrerie.
Photography by Hannah Boquet.

ISBN 979-8-9867143-0-1 (paperback)
ISBN 979-8-9867143-1-8 (ebook)

ALSO BY SANDRINE PILAZ:
Simply French in America – A Guided Journal for Better Family Eating and Lifestyle Habits.

The author can be contacted at sandrine.pilaz@gmail.com

Dedication

*To my four daughters Abigaëlle, Coline, Eléonore and Mathilde.
May you find the power of good food and community.*

Disclaimer

This book is a compilation of my observations and impressions about American food culture and eating habits, after a decade of being a French expat. All the stories I share in this book are based on my experience. They are not substantiated facts, backed up with studies and research.

Some parts of the book are more targeted for parents, specifically moms. Nevertheless, the last chapters about guidelines and recipes are perfect for anyone who wants to do more home cooking.

From time to time, I may seem critical of the SAD (Standard American Diet), however, I never intend to sound condescending or judgmental. Food and eating habits are a very tricky, complicated, and multi-layered topic for discussion. I don't address the systemic issues regarding the way Americans eat: food availability, food deserts, food costs, and economic status. However, I do my best to keep them in mind throughout the book.

I am a holistic health coach and neuropsychologist by training, and a mom of four children. I am not a doctor, a nutritionist, nor a registered dietitian. The information I share is based on my own experiences, learned from my own research. This book is not intended to cure, prevent, diagnose, or treat any disease. Please consult your health care provider regarding any health-related decisions.

Cooking is very subjective. The anticipated outcome of any recipe you create from this book may not always be the one you expect. This can be due to variations in ingredients, humidity, altitude, cooking temperatures, or individual cooking abilities. Don't get discouraged. Keep trying, so you end up adjusting the recipe within your own parameters.

Table of Contents

Preface 13

Introduction 15

PART ONE: My Journey as a French Mom Moving to America ... 21

I am French, so what? 22

Our Honeymoon Phase with America 24

One Hard Thing 28

Food versus Edible Food-Like Substances 30

What Now? 33

PART TWO: Figuring Out My Own Relationship with Food, One Meal at a Time 35

Food to Remember 36

Food Culture 39

Food is Therapeutic 45

Food to Connect 48

Food to Nurture 52

Food Education 56

Live and Eat with Integrity 60

Food to Create Strong Communities 63

Love for Real and Simple Food 66

We Are What We Eat and We Eat What We Are 69

PART THREE: Common Questions and Concerns About Making Food Habits Changes 75

   Why Bother with Home Cooking? 76

   I Don't Have Time to Cook 79

   I Don't Have Any Help 82

   I Am Too Tired 86

   I'm Too Overwhelmed 93

   It is Too Expensive 97

   I Am Not a Good Example for My Kids 104

   I Tried Making Changes But It Never Lasts 108

PART FOUR: Guidelines to Make Home Cooking a Reality 117

   Define Your Home Cooking Style 120

   The Art of a Functional and Practical Kitchen 124

   The Art of Meal Planning: Failing to Plan is Planning to Fail 140

   The Art of Grocery Shopping 150

   The Art of Home Cooking 152

   The Art of Impromptu Cooking 154

   The Art of Healthy Eating 156

   The Art of Raising Healthy Kids 161

   The Art of Peaceful Family Meals 165

   The Art of a Productive Day and the Power of Habits 168

PART FIVE: Recipes 173

   Self-Care "Recipes" 181

Homemade Staples, Toppings, and Tricks That Add Some Magic to Your Cooking and Baking 203

Bread, Pie Crusts, Pizza Dough, and Crepes 229

Breakfast Ideas: Start Your Day Off Right 245

Lunch Ideas: Grab and Go 255

Dinner Ideas: At the Dinner Table 269

Soups and Stews 284

Sweets and Snacks 295

Get to Know Sandrine with Her Favorite Quotes and Mantras That Guide Her Life 309

Additional Reading and Resources: Books, Food Blogs, Websites, & Podcasts 315

Preface

Today is March 20th, 2022. My first book Simply French in America has been a very organic, slow, and long process. I want to be transparent with you right from the start, dear reader. I wrote this preface in a hospital bedroom battling over a severe and debilitating episode of depression/anxiety. And no need to mention that we are living in a time of a pandemic. Two years later, we are still grieving, adapting, and trying to move forward from the Covid-19 pandemic. It is an understatement to say that life can be hard sometimes. Each one of us is facing challenges of our own.

When things get really messy and confusing in my life, one of my coping mechanisms is to simplify as much as I can. I choose to see any challenges I am facing as an opportunity to refocus my attention on what really matters to me. I go back to the basics and discard all the unnecessary. Then I can live with more ease and less overwhelm. To me, those basics come down to three things: shelter to live in, a loving community, and a vibrant, healthy life.

Simply French in America is my humble attempt to weave in these three parameters with an emphasis on good nutrition. Food is our primary fuel for our bodies. I was lucky to grow up in France in the 1980s. So, I benefited from an abundant and rich food culture and food education. Moving to the United States in 2010 had been an eye-opening experience for me as it relates to food. It also sparked the beginning of a more conscious food journey. In this book, I am hoping to give you a whole new perspective on your kitchen space and your cooking skill.

Introduction

One of the most common challenges of parents with young children is providing meals for their families. Life can be hectic and putting a meal together at the end of a long day might not be your favorite thing to do. Why even bother when the American food industry offers instant meal options? Drive-thru's, take-out, eating out, and ordering out have become the norm for families seeking convenience and optimization of their time. Frozen meals, microwavable meals, fast food, and other highly processed options fill refrigerators and pantries with quick and easy alternatives to home cooking. The kitchen doesn't seem to be the heart of the present-day American home anymore, even though food still remains the primary fuel for our bodies. We all need to eat every single day to have the energy to sustain our lives. So, why is such a non-negotiable routine not given more conscious consideration?

My hope is that by sharing my personal insights and simple recipes, you can become more aware of how to use food as a powerful tool to be healthier and connect with your family by bringing mealtimes back into the kitchen. Growing up in France, I learned at an early age that mealtimes and food are vital components of our health. I believe food is medicine because it profoundly affects us physically, mentally, and even on a cellular level. Our health is our most precious asset. It deserves our attention and awareness. Cooking does not have to be complicated or time consuming. My personal motto in all areas of my life is "Keep It Real and Simple." Food and cooking are no exception. This book is meant to be a simple, practical starting point to help you make the changes YOU want around your eating habits. You can pick a few ideas and recipes that interest you, implement them in your daily life, and see how it goes.

Every family is different and what works for one might not work for another. Experience it for yourself and eventually you will follow your own direction, create your personal cookbook, and make your kitchen the place where you and your family go for body, mind, and soul nourishment.

Before we dive in, let me clarify how I define the notions behind the generic term "**health.**" According to the World Health Organization (WHO) website, "Health is a state of complete physical, mental, and social wellbeing, and not merely the absence of disease or infirmity." This is a very broad and vague definition without any guidance on how to achieve that defined state. Scholarly definitions aside, everyone has their own definition of health based on their personal needs and experiences. For some, health is defined by numbers on a weight scale, blood pressure scores, lab work results, or doctor visits. For others, health means following a specific diet or exercise regimen.

Despite the broad spectrum of what health means to each of us, there is one thing we all have in common when it comes to health: we want to feel good. We want sustained energy throughout our day to accomplish what we want/need to do. In that perspective, being healthy is not a destination or a state that we want to achieve, but rather the vehicle on this journey that supports us to live the life we desire. We want to feel our best physically, emotionally, and mentally.

Our health is the most precious foundation for the life we aspire to live fully. I will never forget my grandmother saying "Quand la santé VA, tout VA!" which means "when you are healthy, you have everything." She was so right. Food is your primary fuel for nourishing your body. Every bite you take is a powerful opportunity to promote health or conversely to promote disease.

As for the expression **"Processed Food**," there is a whole spectrum from which a food is considered processed. It is from highly processed items such as beef jerky containing only 10% meat to homemade hummus processed in your food processor. In the context of this book, when I refer to processed food, I am talking about highly processed store-bought items with a long list of low-quality ingredients. It is fair to choose some pre-packaged items to make life easier. But it is essential to look for minimally processed items with high-quality ingredients. In my opinion, processed foods have been designed to get us addicted to them and to disrupt our body wisdom. Body wisdom is an instinctive attraction to the foods that our body needs for nutrition. It tells us exactly what, when, and how much to eat. We all have this intuition, just as animals in the wild do. When you embark on a healthier way of eating, an important point is to reconnect with this inner wisdom and listen to your body. We will cover this aspect later on in this book.

The first two chapters are all about my personal journey as a new mom moving from France to the United States. You will discover my first impressions of the American way of life. I also share about my struggles with adjusting my French way of living and eating when immersed in American culture. From my personal experience, I try to explore the different uses we make from the food we consume. It is pretty obvious that we rarely eat to only fuel our bodies. As social creatures, we often use food to deal with our emotional life or to connect with other people. All those dimensions around eating are worth considering.

The third section of the book is a compilation of the most common concerns I received from families who want to change their eating habits but don't know where to start. We will explore what gets in the way of doing more home cooking: lack of food education/culture, lack of basic cooking skills, lack of time and energy, cost of food, your personal relationship with food, how to get started, and more importantly, how to make those changes last. I will give you enough nuggets of knowledge to chew on so you can make a fresh start and enjoy cooking in your kitchen. I believe this can happen with willingness, awareness, and putting in the work. Therefore, at the end of each question, I encourage you to take action with some practical exercises and reflective questions. I want my words to be a catalyst for change in your life.

Action is the primary focus of the fourth section, as I encourage you to experiment with these suggestions in your kitchen more often. I provide some guidelines for setting up a functional kitchen, meal planning, grocery shopping, food preparation, raising good eaters, and creating successful family meals. There is no right or wrong way to approach this, and I encourage you to try what resonates most with you. Experiment and discover what works for you and your family. Again, feel free to write down your ideas, comments, and questions in the space provided for notes as you are reading through the book. And last but certainly not least, in the last section, I invite you into my kitchen and share the recipes I use every day for my family. Hopefully, some of them will become your favorite dishes as well. You will find some of my favorite French recipes (French baguettes p.232 or crêpes p.241) along with ones with an international flair that I discovered when I moved to the states. The ingredients I use can be found in any local grocery store, cooperative or farmer's market. I do not label my cooking style or affiliate myself with a specific diet. I don't think omitting specific food categories is necessary unless it is medically advised, religiously based or personally derived. In my opinion, excessively restrictive diets don't allow you to develop healthy eating habits that can sustain you for the rest of your life.

All the recipes in this book follow my **SIMPLE** motto:

- **S** hort in time and **S** easonal
- **I** ngredients (10 or less)
- **M** eal plan (it is not as rigid as you think) and **M** oderation
- **P** antry recipes (using basic ingredients you probably already have at home)
- **L** azy cooking (hello one-pot dish, sheet pans and a few dishes to wash after!)
- **E** asy to make (using easy measurement and instructions)

I hope this book inspires you to discover ways to achieve health through food and eating habits that can sustain you and your family for a lifetime. My intentions are to help you take action because it is the only true path to change. Whether you are just beginning your journey to make healthy changes, or you have been traveling the healthy road for a while and would like to add to your culinary repertoire, I aspire to help you. May your journey lead you back to your kitchen with renewed "joie de vivre!" Note: In addition to this book, I created a comprehensive guided journal: *Simply French in America – A Guided Journal for Better Family Eating and Lifestyle Habits*. My intention is to provide you with a helpful, self-reflection tool so you can keep track of the changes you want to make. It would be a good place to gather all your thoughts, resources, questions, and recipes in one place: A perfect companion, alongside this book.

In service and with gratitude, Sandrine.

PART ONE:
My Journey as a French Mom Moving to America

"Life is not about the destination; it is about the journey."
– Ralph Waldo Emerson, essayist, lecturer and poet

I am French, so what?

Thanks to writers such as Pamela Druckerman (Bringing up Bébé), Mireille Guiliano (French Women Don't Get Fat), and Karen LeBillon (French Kids Eat Everything), French moms benefit from a reputation of holistic eating in America. When people in the United States discover I am French, they often assume that I am a good cook and a great parent in all the ways. While these kinds of preconceived ideas made me feel good about myself at first, in reality, it is not that simple and straightforward. Being French doesn't exempt me from struggling to feed myself and my family well during seasons of stress.

Living abroad is a fantastic experience for whoever wants to shake up their habits and get a fresh start. When you live in a foreign country, you can't help but keep comparing it against what you have been familiar with from your native place. It is not necessarily better or worse, but just different. This whirlwind of changes always makes you think hard about all you took for granted or thought was universal. For me, I had this kind of awakening around food and eating habits when I noticed how differently the French consider food compared to Americans. Most French people don't have a passion for cooking. Yet, their intense passion for eating drives them in the kitchen at least twice a day, in a very efficient way, to prepare some simple and impromptu meals. This approach is definitely something that sticks with me after all these years living in the United States.

My expat experience convinces me that where we live in the world doesn't dictate how we eat anymore. Since the beginning of my family's time in the United States, I have been very attached to the idea of giving the best of both American and French cultures to my children. I want to share -the American way of life so my children know that anything and everything is possible, along with some French traditions, especially around food habits like the importance of using real and simple ingredients when cooking combined with regular mealtimes. Everyone can apply some aspects of a French lifestyle and make it work while living in the U.S. Learning to fit into America's society while maintaining and transferring my French roots has been an interesting journey for me. A journey which I am excited to share with you. It all began with our move overseas and, subsequently, our honeymoon phase with America.

Our Honeymoon Phase with America

My journey towards being more aware and conscious around food probably began when I moved to the U.S. from France with my family on August 24, 2010. At that time, my husband got a post-doctoral position at Johns Hopkins University in Baltimore, Maryland. This big move overseas was a huge milestone for our family. Newly married, as we celebrated our first anniversary on August 22, 2009, we had at that time two daughters, ages five months and seventeen months old. We took a giant leap of faith, got rid of all our belongings, and left our French family and friends to live out this new, big adventure. Neither of us had experience living abroad. We arrived at the international airport in Baltimore with our life packed in four simple

suitcases and our two daughters in baby carriers. (Somehow, I managed to put my big and heavy cast-iron skillet in our luggage, evidence that cooking was already a priority). We were ready to start over, in a foreign country, with a foreign language, without our family or friends.

I wanted and needed this change. It was like having a second chance to build the life I really wanted., Putting some geographical distance from my past, with its challenges and traumas, is exactly what I needed. And to be honest, my husband and I liked the idea of doing something different from the majority of our generation (going to college, getting a job, finding a partner, getting married, buying a house close to family, etc.). We were lucky to share this craving for adventure together. Leaving everything behind us and starting from scratch a new life abroad? Hell yes! It was kind of foolish to think that I would be able to handle anything and be the person I have always wanted to be (even though I didn't even have a clear picture of what this person would look like). And yet, I was pretty excited about this new chapter in our lives.

I convinced myself that it shouldn't be that hard to acclimate to American culture. After all, it is not like we were moving to the Eastern part of the world, where the cultural shock and language acquisition would have been more dramatic. After many late nights figuring out logistics around deadlines for paperwork, the endless to-do lists, and the mental preparation that goes into moving two infants across the world, we finally made it safely to Baltimore, Maryland. Our honeymoon phase with America was in full swing, and I loved it! Over the first few weeks after our move, I was fascinated and curious about all the different aspects between French and American culture. I had my camera with me everywhere I went to capture every exotic detail. Then, I was rushing to my computer to share my experience on my French blog (6OutWest.com) for my family and friends in France to follow along on this journey. Here are some of my first impressions about America after just a few weeks of being immersed in Baltimore:

First of all, **the people were so friendly**. I will always remember the very first time I went for a stroll in our neighborhood. Every person I passed whose eyes I met asked me, "How are you?" It was so unreal for me with my French roots. If we were to do that in France, people would automatically get suspicious of your intentions. They would ask if we knew each other, or worse, they would simply ignore you. Sad, but true!

Not only were people super friendly with me, but they were also charming with my kids. **We moved to a very kid-friendly culture**! In France, you almost avoid public places and grocery stores when you have kids with you, fearing critical comments and judgements. They have to behave properly to be tolerated in those types of locations. Here in the U.S., wherever we went, my kids were always welcomed. From the cashier or shoppers at the grocery store to the doctor's office or the banker, they all paid attention to my children. They interacted with them in such a genuine and friendly way. I could bring them anywhere! It was so convenient. My only complaint, though, was the "food"-rewarding aspect of those encounters. It is very common to see a merchant, a doctor, or a banker offering food samples, candy, lollipops, or mints to the kids. I get it: American businesses want to be remembered. But why do they have to connect with their clientele using cheap, sugary treats? What does it say about the relationship they want to build?

One other thing that struck me about the U.S. is an **overall positive mindset**. I have to say, I love it! There is genuine optimism. Americans have this sense that everything is possible as long as you stay enthusiastic and work hard. The American life coach, Marie Forleo, sums it up very well with her famous tweet that became a book. "Everything is Figuroutable." In France, it is quite the opposite philosophy, with the idea that nothing is possible in the first place. I like Henry Miller's quote on this matter: "In America, every man is potentially president. Here in France, every man is potentially a zero." But in my opinion, there is a flip side to this idea of self-determination. There is this near obsession with willpower: If you fail, it's because you are weak. If you are struggling, you ought to push harder. If you are craving something not good for you, you have to resist.

Americans have grown accustomed to the belief that their will alone is what makes things happen. For me, this approach is not sustainable or healthy. Yes, willpower is meant to get us through difficult moments and challenging situations, but the negative self-talk that often comes with this mindset can be problematic if we are not aware of it. **Americans can be very hard on themselves.**

Everything was definitely bigger and larger here in America, from the fridge and washing machine and dryer to the cars and roads, and even bottles of milk or orange juice. I felt like a Lilliputian – very small or trivial- in a world of giants. Nevertheless, it was something we got used to quickly. We were still enjoying living in a straightforward and minimalist way. Still, we also appreciated all the space and comforts we had living here in America.

Those first weeks of immersion in a foreign country were so memorable and fun. Lots of things were different from what I was used to in France. **It wasn't necessarily better or worse but just different**. I just loved observing and noticing those contrasts between these two worlds. Overall, I felt very open to discovering a new culture. Still, there was one aspect of American culture that I had a tough time embracing. By the point, I am pretty sure it is obvious to you, dear reader, on what that one thing was!

One Hard Thing

Food was definitely my biggest challenge in terms of adjusting to this new American culture. Everything related to food was different from what I was exposed to in France. All of the usual questions around food immediately arose – what, where, when, why, and how should I eat.

Before I dive into what bothered me, I have to note that I also have great memories of eating in the U.S. We ate sizzling hamburgers and decadent pizzas during the first weeks following our move. I also went to the local library trying to find cookbooks that would provide me with the best chocolate cookie and brownie recipes, knowing there would be aisles and aisles of sweets to shop from at the grocery store. But I got bored quickly and my waistline wasn't very happy either after gaining some extra pounds. After just a few weeks, I was left with a sugar hangover and lots of mixed feelings about our food options.

I didn't have the same openness and curiosity regarding this aspect of American culture as I had for the others. **I found myself being harsh, critical, and judgmental**. I discovered a totally different world from grocery stores to food courts in malls to TV food-ads and eating habits. Before moving, our French friends were teasing us that we would live in the country that eats the most fast-food in the world. We lived in Lyon, sometimes described as the "world capital of gastronomy." It was quite a shock to come from a French foodie town filled with amazing outdoor markets and restaurants to a place where the heavy, grease-slung options at fast-food restaurants are the norm.

Junk food was now the easiest option and most available at any time. I was so surprised to observe the lengthy drive-in line at a fast-food restaurant in the middle of the afternoon or to see people scarfing down a slice of pizza in their car in the middle of the morning, or kids having goldfish crackers for a snack (those goldfish are everywhere and available any time of day). It seemed there was no specific time during the day for eating. We had a glimpse of that lifestyle from the American movies. Still, it was another story when it became part of your direct environment. This time, it was real and not so funny! I didn't anticipate and measure the impact this way of eating has on culture and vice versa. Even if you make it a point to not support the fast-food industry, you are inundated with food ads from mail and television and brightly colored signs that fill almost every main street. **Eating out and ordering take-out is a big part of American food culture**. It is not just for a special occasion but more like a weekly routine. However, I like to know the ingredients of the food I eat and how it was prepared, so we didn't pick up this habit upon our move to the United States.

I soon discovered it would require more time, more energy, and more profound research to create meals for my family that I would be satisfied to serve them. I guess the honeymoon phase of our expatriation was over. Time to regroup, think hard, and get down to the nitty-gritty of our new life abroad.

Food versus Edible Food-Like Substances

Our very first trip to an American grocery store was quite an adventure! Certainly, it was an experience I will never forget. I didn't have a clue about what the supermarket industry looked like in the U.S. I went to the closest mainstream supermarket near our house. It is an understatement to say that it was an overwhelming and challenging experience. **I felt so lost wandering up and down the aisles, seeing the abundance of different and new brands**. And even when I found a familiar product such as a Danone yogurt, the package and the product itself were different from what we used to buy in France. The container was much larger in size, and the list of ingredients also varied uncomfortably from the French version. For instance, gelatin is often used in American yogurts to give consistency and texture to the product, whereas French yogurts do not.

I noticed that the most oversized aisles in U.S. stores are for chips, bread, soda, cereals, and snacks (so mostly packaged and processed foods). Those large aisles usually occupy the middle of the stores. My first instinctive reaction was to stay close to the fresh produce aisles traditionally located around the perimeter of the store (at the entrance for fruits and vegetables and all the way across for milk, cheese, and eggs). I didn't venture much into the middle of the supermarket where all the processed food was located. I was already aware of this marketing strategy to force people to wander in the store, hoping they would buy something they haven't planned on their way to get the milk. But they couldn't fool me!

When I wandered in the middle of the store aisles, **I started freaking out looking at the labels**. I couldn't read them- not because my English wasn't good, but because of all the names of chemicals, fillers, and additives used. Michael Pollan's book, *Food Rules: An Eater's Manual*, sums it up very well: "Food in mainstream markets is not food but edible food-like substances. There are highly processed concoctions designed by food scientists, consisting mostly of ingredients derived from corn and soy, and containing chemical additives." More and more, we hear the term "Frankenfood" to describe food that has been genetically modified. For example, a loaf of bread made with Monsanto® wheat, or a tomato that has been modified to improve its ability to travel to the grocery store without bruising.

That day, **I left the store with some carrots, potatoes, tomatoes, milk, eggs, butter, flour, and mozzarella, but most of all, with tons of questions**!

I clearly remember saying to myself: "That is not food!! Why are the lists of ingredients so long? Why were most of the products enriched in all kinds of vitamins and other types of additives? Why do they put paraben in a baguette? Why are eggs and milk refrigerated? What is sour cream versus whipping cream? Why is there a small aisle called "Health Food?" Does it mean that the rest of the store is filled with crap?" If only I had known Estelle Tracy, another French expat, who had the same struggle as I did. She wrote a booklet to help French expats navigate the U.S. supermarkets (it's called *Le guide de survie alimentaire aux Etats-Unis - The survival food guide in the U.S.*). Had I read the book prior to the move, my experience would probably have been different and less overwhelming.

What Now?

This very first exposure to an American grocery store left me very perplexed. It made me wonder how Americans define food. Is it only something they put into their mouth to get some immediate satisfaction, without any second thought on what they are feeding to their bodies and the consequences it can have? Why is junk food so prevalent? Before moving to a foreign country, it never occurred to me that the simple act of eating was weaved into so many different aspects of life. My first few months of expatriation were so eye opening in that regard. I got to personally explore some complicated layers around eating. In hindsight, I came to realize that there were so many different ways one can approach food. Depending on what season in life you are in, where you live, your upbringing, the food culture you are exposed to, your economic status, or your level of stress, you will consider food and the simple act of eating in very different ways. It strikes me that the English language has so many words related to eating: eating, feeding, binging, nourishing, and nurturing. I especially appreciate the distinction between eating and feeding. The former is related to consuming food without much thought beyond its taste. It feeds your belly. That's it. While the latter implies making deliberate food choices based on our needs. It nourishes a deeper layer of our being. I am very excited to share with you my food journey and see what it stirs up for you.

PART TWO:
Figuring Out
My Own Relationship with
Food,
One Meal at a Time

"Your Diet Is a Bank Account. Good Food Choices Are Good Investments."
– Bethenny Frankel, reality television personality and entrepreneur

Food to Remember

Despite all the excitement associated with living in a new place, I started feeling homesick. I missed my family and friends in France. We had no support for raising our daughters. I also felt some isolation due to my limited English. I noticed that I started craving the comfort food I grew up with quiches, crêpes, croque-monsieur, yogurt cake, clafoutis, baguettes, and good cheese. This time of nostalgia brought back so many food memories from my childhood. Luckily, I brought in my luggage a precious notebook that I started when I was dating my husband. In it, I carefully wrote down all of my favorite recipes. I remember my grandma and my mom had kept similar handwritten heirloom recipes. Passing them on from generation to generation is a priceless tradition in most French families. I was so glad to have brought this notebook with me and felt the need to use it now more than ever.

Nevertheless, my first experiments to replicate some French recipes proved to be a total disaster. I had to deal with different kitchen devices and different measurements. Where are my grams, kilograms, liters, Celsius? Instead, I had to get used to ounces, pounds, gallons, cups, teaspoons, tablespoons, and Fahrenheit. I will never forget my first attempt to bake a simple yogurt cake. Yogurt cake is a staple in France. It is the first cake a child learns to bake. Well, my first American kitchen venture at baking a yogurt cake was a disaster. The cake was just inedible. I may have done something wrong with how I measured out the quantities of the ingredients. But also, the basic ingredients such as flour, yeast, eggs, and yogurt were simply different. It took me a while to feel comfortable and at ease in my American kitchen. But, little by little, with lots of trials and errors, I learned to replicate my French recipes into our new American life.

What helped me tremendously during those first months of expatriation was that my French education around food had been good enough to not fall into some common pitfalls. Being in a new (and sort of hostile and unsafe) food environment, it was as if I needed to reactivate this knowledge and bring it back to my consciousness. Indeed, it is such a big part of French culture that we don't even have to think about it. It is like second nature. The principle of consuming food that fuels you and food that is real and delicious is so deeply rooted in French culture. I never would have thought that this concept wasn't universal around the world. It was such a big realization for me to accept that not everyone lives with these guidelines. I know I was kind of naive and self-centered to think this. I guess it is one of the numerous advantages of traveling and discovering new cultures. Being far from my native country was the moment when I really understood the singularity of the French way of eating.

*****

Food for Thought

Food has a way of evoking our own past and reminding us of who we are and where we are from. Whether the food tastes good to us or not, it is deeply connected with our memories, good and bad. Maybe you grew up with industrial frozen meals and canned food. And you keep holding on to happy meals and powdered orange macaroni and cheese, because those tastes are tied so firmly to your past and they are what you are familiar with. The memories that are attached with the food are much more important than the food itself.

Note: I want to point out that before the revolution of packaged food, North American and European foods were more alike than different in a few fundamental ways. There was no chemical fertilizer or pesticides on North American farmlands when those areas were first being settled. There were no chemical additives and preservatives. The food was grown and raised locally, and most of it was prepared and consumed at home.

- ✓ Do you have any food memories that rise to the surface as you are reading this section?
- ✓ What food or dishes do you remember from your childhood that you would like to make again?
- ✓ Do you know your family history? What is your family heritage? Do you have recipes from your ancestors before the era of packaged foods?

....
....
....
....
....
....
....

✳✳✳✳

Food Culture

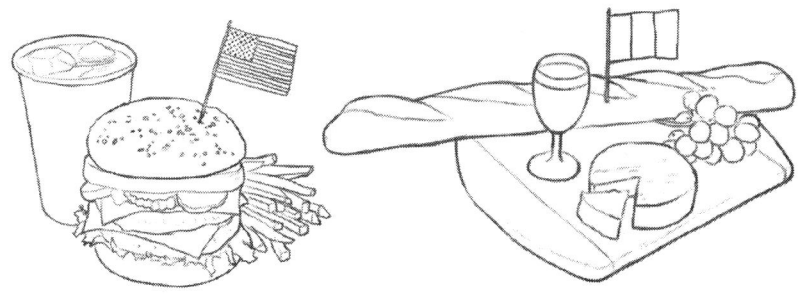

Weeks passed, and we started making deeper connections with some American families. I intentionally wanted to get to know those people better around a good meal because I consider food to be one of the best ways to show our love and connection with each other. **Those first experiences as a host were very instructive.** Of course, I made lots of mistakes along the way because of my lack of knowledge about American eating habits. My first hesitation was about time. **What time do I invite guests to come over?** I had noticed that Americans eat dinner much earlier than French. There was no way we could tell people to come over at 7:00 p.m. But at the same time, starting to eat at 5:00 p.m. was really not an option for me. We just had the four o'clock snack (Le fameux goûter). And do they have "l'apéritif"? (a time when we gather before the meal to enjoy an alcoholic drink with some appetizers). To what extent could we use our French eating habits in the U.S. while respecting our guests' own eating habits?

I also needed to think about the type of food I would offer. I have noticed that American people are used to introducing themselves by mentioning their type of diet (vegetarian, vegan, paleo, gluten-free, nut-free, or dairy-free diet, anyone?). **They like to identify themselves with what they can eat but most of all with what they cannot eat!** When food is involved, you always have to ask the question about food allergies and preferences. It is part of the "American welcoming protocol." I don't remember food allergies being so prevalent in France.

The first big holiday we got to celebrate in America after our move was Thanksgiving. It was an important discovery for us since we don't have an equivalent holiday in France. Thanksgiving is one of the favorite holidays among Americans. While it can be a very stressful time of the year, marking the start of the winter holiday season, with lots of travel and gift exchanges, this holiday is mostly a time of gratitude and connection. Thanksgiving is all about family gathering, taking the time to be grateful for all the resources one has, and, of course, sharing a good meal with lots of food. It is supposed to be a very joyful time. Unfortunately, I keep hearing people complaining about how much food they ate and how bad they felt right after, leading to a week of caloric deprivation.

French do have some big meals too, especially around big holidays and special events such as weddings, birthdays, family gatherings, or family Sunday lunches. Meals can last hours, with animated discussions and lots of laughs. We take the time to enjoy every bite of food and every sip of wine. This slow pace gives us time to digest between dishes (also, we have new plates for each new dish, so the table setting reinforces the ritual). **The notion of pleasure and enjoyment is really palpable and central in France**. From the moment you prepare the food in your kitchen, this notion is everywhere: the decorations on the table (nice silverware and napkins), the presentation of the food, the taste, the smell, and the good company. I didn't really get this feeling during our first Thanksgiving. Everything felt rushed. All the food was at the table in a potluck style, and we were just filling our plates until they were totally covered with food, one dish blending into the next. Instead of connecting with each other, talking, and sharing stories, the TV was the main entertainment, even when eating. This experience was so different from what I had experienced in France when we shared a meal. Again, it was an interesting contrast to notice and to be aware of during this transitional phase.

Here is a comparative chart about my observations of American and French food culture.

FRANCE	*USA*
• Strong national food culture heritage	• No real national food identity, but rather a multicultural nation (Mexican, Italian, Thai, Chinese, Vietnamese, Lebanese…) • Americans are exposed to a bigger variety of food but with no unified sets of eating rules
• Solid framework in terms of what, when, and how to eat • People will take a poor view of someone who doesn't partake of the main dish or only eats gluten-free foods • What counts most of all is conviviality	• Americans are more entitled to eat differently • Loose frame
• Culinary conception of food • Importance of traditional wisdom: Sense of smell, taste, and texture are essential • Eat food for fuel AND also for pleasure and enjoyment	• Scientific and nutritional conception of food Americans don't see the food for itself but rather the nutrients it contains ("Eat a banana because it is rich in potassium") • Focus more on health and wellbeing, importance of vitamins, supplements and fortified foods
• National consensus regarding daily eating times (Breakfast around 7:30am, Lunch around noon, goûter around 4pm and Dinner around 7:30pm) • No snacking in between meals • Food is a collective concern, almost a form of communion	• More of a snacking culture. Americans tend to eat when they feel hungry, anytime during the day • Not a really specific time dedicated to meals at a table • Everyone eats at their own speed, outside constraints and timetable. It is not a social activity

FRANCE	USA
<ul><li>The French take their time when they eat</li><li>No multitasking</li><li>Everybody sits at a table</li><li>Meals are strongly associated with good company and sharing. There is something sacred about meals. It doesn't feel quite right to eat alone</li></ul>	<ul><li>Americans are champions at multitasking</li><li>They don't mind eating while doing other things: eating in front of the computer, eating while walking to get to the next appointment, or eating while driving is very common</li><li>Family meals at a dining table are not the norm</li></ul>
<ul><li>Breakfast and afternoon snacks (le goûter) are usually sweet</li><li>Cereals with milk, bread with butter and jam, hot cocoa/orange juice, for breakfast, and fruits with a biscuit for an afternoon goûter</li></ul>	<ul><li>More options for breakfast. Americans are willing to cook breakfast, if they make time for it</li><li>Savory breakfast is common too (eggs and bacon, anyone?)</li><li>Also, savory options for snacks (veggie sticks with hummus, cheese with crackers…)</li></ul>
<ul><li>Soft drinks are just for special occasions.</li><li>Water is the first drink</li><li>No milk during mealtime, except for breakfast with cereals or for an occasional hot chocolate</li></ul>	<ul><li>Milk is often offered for lunch and dinner in the US</li><li>Sodas are common beverages any time of the day and during meals as well</li></ul>
<ul><li>Supermarkets are commonplace, but there are still many places with local shops such as butcheries (boucheries), fish shops (poissonneries), cheese shops (fromageries) and of course bakeries (boulangeries)</li><li>Farmers markets are popular and quite an experience</li></ul>	<ul><li>Big box stores (Target, Walmart…) are the norm</li><li>No bakeries at every corner. Less temptation to stop by and buy bread or pastries</li><li>Some farmers markets but not as impressive as the ones in France</li></ul>

The food in France is more than something to eat. It is embedded in our lives. Like Jeannie Marshall shared beautifully in her book, *The Lost Art of Feeding Kids,* "[food] is a simple pleasure on the surface, but one that is in reality a complex web of history, place, religion, family, health, community." A food culture has something to do with recipes and ingredients but also rules and structure. It offers solid eating habits instead of allowing grazing, nibbling, and snacking all day long. Because North America is a nation of immigrants, individuals and families don't have this solid common ground. Each American has to rediscover a personal and family food culture on their own.

After World War II, the United States entered a new modern age of innovation that profoundly changed the way that America cooked and ate. The revolution of packaged food in the 1950s combined with a more scientific approach to food, led to a food culture dictated by the food industry. **Big American food corporations have become the health authority for this country**. They have inserted themselves between the child and the parents.

American food industry has convinced parents that:
- Cooking is a waste of time and not a valuable skill to have and transmit to our children.
- Processed foods will actually nourish our children. The health claims on children's breakfast cereals and other food products appeal to parents' intellect. We all want our children to grow up healthy and strong, so we are more likely to choose foods that promise to promote health and strength.
- Food marketers are willing to spend millions of dollars on labeling with very convincing and manipulative health claims.

Note about Food Insecurity in North America: Food insecurity is when you do not have reliable access to adequate nutritious food or lack the resources to purchase it. It is definitely a complex and systemic issue with racial, cultural, and socioeconomic roots, that I won't address here. There is a good proportion of American families relying on convenience stores or dollar stores to get their groceries, with mostly highly processed foods for long life-shelf purpose. At the end of the day, they might have to travel miles through heavy traffic to get to the grocery store. But there's usually a fast-food restaurant nearby that will resolve all the dinner struggles (no cooking, no cleaning, and kids are happy). When money and time are already stretched thin, it's easy for a more nutritious diet to fall off the priority list.

Generally speaking, access to fresh and real food is better in France. But French families with lower income have a tendency to reach for more affordable items such as high caloric foods (cereals, sweets, and added fats) instead of nutrient-rich sources of food. That being said, most French families still take the time to cook dinners.

****

Food for Thought

- ✓ What does this comparison bring to the surface for you?
- ✓ What are your eating habits?
- ✓ Do you agree with my perception of American food culture?
- ✓ Reading suggestion: *Unsavory Truth: How Food Companies Skew The Science of What We Eat* by Marion Nestle.

....
....
....
....
....
....
....
....
....
....
....
....
....
....
....

****

Food is Therapeutic

Five months after our move overseas, **I got pregnant with our third baby. Three babies in three years.** Oh my! To be honest, it is an understatement to say that it was a stressful and tiring time for me. Having to begin a new pregnancy while away from my family and friends, in a foreign country, with no knowledge of the American health-care system was quite challenging. One said it takes a village to raise a child. At that time, it felt like less of a village and more of a rudimentary campsite. It came down to just my husband and I for the care of our family. All of our loved ones were in France, and I made the terrible mistake to not ask for support from my American acquaintances. I didn't feel like I knew them well enough to open myself up and share my struggles. Plus, I was the only one expecting a third baby. They all had one or two babies at that time, and we were all trying to keep our heads above water during those first intense years of parenting. I didn't ask for help, assuming it would be too much for them to lend a hand. So, during those nine months, I was in autopilot mode, day after day, trying to survive in this motherhood world on my own.

In retrospect, I realize now that I was depressed and not happy with my life. I have opted to raise my daughters following the attachment parenting philosophy, which emphasizes close physical contact and loving attunement to their physical and emotional needs. But it was so demanding to be present for them and fulfill their needs all day long, in a culture different from the one I grew up in, and with very limited support. I was missing a key aspect to thriving as a stay-home mom. **In trying to provide constant loving care, I didn't dedicate enough time for self-care, compassion, and loving-kindness toward myself**. It is probably the biggest lesson I learned from that period of my life.

And so, I began to feel severely depressed. I had so much to carry every day – literally and figuratively. I was holding and gestating three little lives with my one and unsupported body. I totally neglected those feelings and just kept moving forward no matter what. **I wanted to have everything under control, from the food I chose for my family to the way I gave birth to my third child**. I decided to have a home birth for my third daughter. This choice was certainly part of that desire to be in charge and in control. This way, I didn't have to deal with American hospitals and their highly medicated protocols. However, the negative effect of having a home birth when you don't have a community to support you is that you end up going back to your daily life too quickly. So, within hours of the birth, life was exactly the way it was before, only this time I had my precious newborn in my arms. It is hard to articulate how chaotic my inner world became, and I am afraid it resulted from me saying yes to too much. Only a couple hours after I gave birth to Eléonore, I was standing in my kitchen baking a birthday cake for my three-year-old daughter,

Abigaëlle. I am not proud of that. For many years that followed, I felt a lot of shame for not slowing down and asking for help. Being able to put words for how I felt during that time, I came to this big realization that **as much as I was a restless and tired mom, cooking and eating was the only moment during the day where it was my turn to be mothered and not the other way around**. Yes, I was cooking for my family, and it was a lot of work. But because I was in charge, I chose the food I was enjoying for myself. It gave me so much pleasure to eat food that I love. In some ways, **cooking and eating was an act of self-love in disguise.** Food took care of me. I felt nourished and nurtured. Because of our life circumstances at that time (no family or friends around, newly arrived in a foreign country), I used cooking and eating as my coping mechanism to keep going. It was my primary fuel on all levels.

****

Food for Thought

- ✓ What is your relationship with food?
- ✓ What do you use food for?
- ✓ Do you look to food to comfort or to fill a void?

....
....
....
....
....
....
....
....

****

Food to Connect

After about a year in Baltimore, we just started to feel settled in our new life. Coincidentally, the day I was expressing this feeling to my husband, we learned that the lab he was working in would be closing in a couple of months. It was quite a shock; we were totally unprepared for that kind of news. The picture was not very appealing: **no more work, a stressed and scared dad, a sleep-deprived and depressed mom with two toddlers and a three-week-old baby, in a foreign country.** I was devastated and more depressed than ever. My hormones were a wreck. I was at the mercy of my emotions and found myself crying, food binging, and doubting a lot. Fortunately, my husband found another post-doc position a few months later. We were able to get our act together, and we kept moving on with our life. Durham, North Carolina, here we come!

Time to pack again. This time, all our belongings were held in a small moving truck, heading South to Durham. After fourteen months spent at Johns Hopkins, my husband started a new post-doctoral position at Duke University. A new chapter in our lives was about to begin. We discovered the Southern part of the United States, and we enjoyed it a lot. This new environment was a better fit for our family's lifestyle, being closer to nature, surrounded by forests, parks, and camping opportunities. I immediately fell in love with Durham. It had a great vibe. We found it to be very progressive, with tons of creative and inspiring people. **For the first time in my life, I felt deeply that I was in the right place at the right time.** What a wonderful feeling! I didn't know what kind of opportunities I would embrace yet, but I felt confident that good things were bound to happen here. Over the last couple of years, Durham has seen an incredible mixture of chefs, farmers, brewers, and bakers who have quietly transformed the city into one of the hottest food destinations in the South. The "Bull City" has so many culinary treasures to offer. It was so good to move to a place where people have the same interest and love for tasty foods. Farmers markets, good restaurants, CSAs (Community-Supported Agriculture), food trucks, and different associations to end hunger constitute a significant part of Durham's identity and became part of our family's weekly schedule.

Another aspect that made Durham so special was that we found it to be a cosmopolitan town. Duke University attracts so many international students and families from all over the world, which organically forms a richly diverse community. I made some truly amazing friends during our eight years in Durham. They are a big part of who I have become today. As a matter of fact, **my international friends helped me widen my culinary horizon**. I enjoyed meeting moms from Japan or India every week to exchange recipes and tips in the kitchen. It was so interesting to have the same goal (feeding our family with healthy food) but using different approaches and ingredients as well as different cultures and knowledge, from Macrobiotic to Ayurvedic. We were learning so much from each other. **My American friends inspired me in other ways too. They helped me discover new ways of cooking**. It appeared that most of them (and/or members of their families) had some sort of food allergies. They were trying so hard to be creative in the kitchen for the wellness of their families. I wanted to find nutritious recipes for them when they were invited to share a meal with us. There might be good cooks in France, but most of them cook in a very traditional way (using dairy and wheat as the main base). Food intolerances and food allergies are not that prevalent in France, as compared to the United States. Therefore, other alternatives such as gluten-free, vegetarian, vegan, dairy-free, paleo, AIP (auto-immune protocol) dishes are less prevalent there. Food allergies/intolerances are so common in the U.S. that you have to learn to cook food from different repertoires if you want to invite friends over for dinner. We are lucky to not have any food allergies in our house. I feel very grateful to have had that opportunity to be exposed to so many different "diets." Today, with the expansion of the food blogosphere, it is easier than ever to get some inspiration and create new recipes that my family and friends can enjoy (even though I didn't like this whole dieting thing and labeling my food). **My only criteria for the food I chose to cook was that it had to be quick, simple, tasty, and appreciated by my family and guests.** I realized that most of the connections I made at that time (whether with my American or international friends) were related to food and cooking. Food is truly an amazing and wonderful vector of connection, no matter the culture you live in. I would even say that **food is the ultimate connector**. It connects us to each other AND to our bodies.

****

Food for Thought

- ✓ Do you see how food can help you connect with your family and other people in your community?

- ✓ Do you like to host dinner or potlucks at your house? Do you have a favorite dish you like to make for those occasions?
- ✓ Do you remember any of your friendships starting around a food story?

****

Food to Nurture

Durham might have been the perfect place to raise my daughters and have tons of outdoor adventures and outstanding culinary experiences. However, I was still a full-time stay-at-home mom with three kids under four to care for seven days a week, with a husband working many hours to establish himself in his field. So, I tried to make the best of my situation as an expat-stay-at-home mom. It didn't make sense for me to go back to "work" (for pay, that is). Even if I wanted to, it would have been very complicated. As a neuropsychologist in France, I couldn't practice here in the U.S. without going back to university and getting a new degree. Instead, I progressively made peace with the idea of not being fully active in the professional world, and **I decided to focus on taking care of my family and exploring my passion for cooking homemade meals**. Unlike some people who love to eat out and have a break from cooking, I love to stay home and cook whatever I have on hand. I love to go to my friends' homes and hang out, poking into their cupboards if they let me. I enjoy learning about their favorite recipes and cooking experiences. The best way to create my personal recipe repertoire is to collect the best tips and recipes from my direct community.

I was in a constant quest for inspiration and recipes to please each family member. Here were my criteria: easy and quick to prepare, using simple ingredients, and tasty and kids-approved! I wanted recipes that I could use over and over again. It wasn't an easy task, though. Each of my daughters has their own food preferences. One has been vegetarian and dairy-free since she started eating solid food. Another loves meat and could only eat this. And one is not a big fan of vegetables, so I have to develop creative ways to get some in her diet. I had more failures than successes. I felt discouraged many times. I had many days where I put a lot of energy into finding new recipes, trying them out in my kitchen, and all I got from my kids at the end was a big "Yuck, I won't give it a try!" But I persisted. In retrospect, **I realized that cooking was actually what kept me from debilitating depression**. It was my way of getting out of my daily struggles and negative self-talk pattern. There were days when I felt tired and very depressed. Nonetheless, you would still find me in my tiny, windowless galley kitchen, cooking every day. This was my go-to place to refill my cup. It was becoming a passion: a passion I felt more and more the need to share with my direct community.

My daughters became old enough to start preschool, attend birthday parties, and participate in different sports activities. This meant **the beginning of a never-ending exposure to other living and eating ways that were very different from what we were trying to implement at home**. I was trying very hard to implement basic healthy food habits in our household. But I no longer had total control over the foods my kids were consuming. It was so hard for me to be ok watching them eat "Franken-food"! Basically, every time we left the house, I experienced stress and anxiety because they were exposed to food that did not meet my standards. I began to wonder if it was even possible to raise my kids the "French way" in an American environment, where the snacking culture is omnipresent. A simple trip to the playground could turn into a hassle because my daughters wanted to have food that the other kids were having, no matter the time of the day.

This period challenged me to step back and reconsider my approach around feeding my family. It was getting to a point where mealtime became miserable, loaded with anxiety, frustration, and stress. I wanted to control everything. In doing so, my ever-present fear negatively impacted my husband and daughters, spoiling our time together. My daughters didn't want to help me in the kitchen. They didn't feel welcome as they felt my anxiety around cooking healthy food. I went too far with my desire to feed my family properly. My passion became an obsession, and I started falling into some orthorexia. **I forgot all about the pleasure of eating. I made it too much of a big deal. Simplicity, connection, and joy were lost for the sake of health.** It was all about me cooking and healing. And at that time, I didn't focus my attention and energy on simply educating my kids around food so they can, in turn, make smart decisions on their own when I am not with them.

****

Food for Thought

- ✓ How do you feel about preparing meals for your family?
- ✓ Is cooking a pleasure or a burden?
- ✓ Do you educate your children around food and eating habits?
- ✓ Do your children help in the kitchen? Do they participate in the meal plan and meal prep? Do they cook?

....
....
....
....

****

Food Education

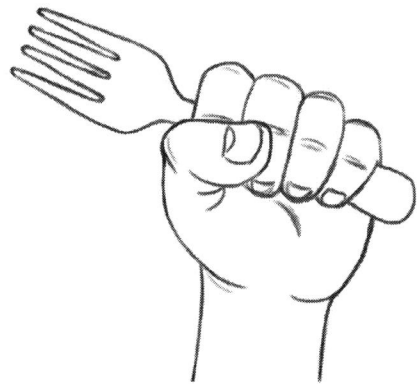

I had some sort of relief when I realized that I wasn't the only one feeling stressed around feeding my family. I met so many American moms in distress, desperately wanting to feed their children better food than a frozen packaged meal. They were looking for simple basics in the kitchen so they could offer decent options to their families. They wanted to make positive changes, but the problem was that they didn't know where to start. I also noticed that some parents didn't initiate changes, fearing negative comments for not following the mainstream ("I would love to bring something healthier for my child's birthday at his preschool, but what will everyone think if I don't bring cupcakes with lots of icing? What if kids don't like the snack I brought? Will they make fun of my child?").

From chatting with lots of moms at playgrounds, the question that brought the most daily despair was, "What are we going to have for dinner?" Most of the time, they would say: "I don't really feel like making anything, so I guess I am going to choose take out or defrost a pizza." Feeling the distress and the needs of those moms was a turning point for me. There is an in-between solution in my opinion, using real and simple food and not spending two hours in the kitchen. I felt compelled to share simple tips, guidelines, recipes, and basic cooking skills to shift their perception around feeding their families. Since I was experiencing this daily with my own family, I knew exactly what it felt like to be stressed out around dinnertime, with the pressure to provide nutritious dishes. It was so gratifying to help come up with tailored meals for each of these families. For the first time in my life, I felt confident and strong enough to share my point of view regarding eating habits no matter anyone's opinion. I was too passionate to stay silent. So, despite my French accent and fear of public speaking, slowly but surely, I started speaking up about the importance of eating real food and sharing a meal with other people.

All those experiences led me to a shift in my career. In 2015, I became an Integrative Health Coach with the Institute for Integrative Nutrition. This training gave me the confidence I lacked to share my story. I am now dedicated to helping moms make lifestyle changes that produce real and lasting results. I have always seen myself as a lifelong learner, but I didn't anticipate that this first training in the U.S. will bring so much personal growth. Studying health coaching and food with an "American mindset" was both an exciting and disturbing journey for my family and myself, to say the least. Among other things, I learned about more than a hundred dietary theories. I wasn't aware of most of them because I didn't grow up in a dieting culture (South Beach diet, Atkins diet, Dukan diet, low-fat diet, cabbage soup diet, grapefruit diet, I could go on and on…). Every time I was learning about a new dietary theory from the world's top experts, I was, at first, seduced and kind of convinced about the benefits from each of those diets. Each guest speaker, who was a leader in his field, was so persuasive! Being that I was also on a personal quest to discover which foods were best for my body, I wanted to experiment with some of those diets. It was also part of the school assignment: During a whole year, every month, we were asked to experiment with a new food trend: vegetarian, vegan, less sugar, more or less fat... And this is how I fell into this rabbit hole of a dieting mindset ("I shouldn't eat this even if I like it, I should be eating this even if I don't like it"). This attitude did not align with my French food education and the way I feel about eating habits. It was confusing. As a good student, I wanted to do my homework well, and my intentions were good. Still, I was stress-driven and surely wasn't going anywhere experimenting like this. All these myriads of diets helped me realize that the solution to eating better can't be found in books or in following a so-called food expert. We have to figure it out by ourselves using our common sense and self-awareness.

The silver lining of this health coaching training experience is that I experienced this dieting environment that most American moms experience daily. I felt like I got to put myself into their shoes to some extent. It also helped me bring more awareness and mindfulness around my eating habits, which is the first step toward making changes. And that's when a health coach can come in handy. Having a professional on your side can be of tremendous help when you want to change your eating habits.

A **DIE**ting mindset	A **LIFE**style mindset
<ul><li>Short term vision</li><li>Often a weight loss goal in mind (counting calories)</li><li>There is good and bad food</li><li>Nutrition facts are essential</li><li>Using supplements to cover up a bad diet</li><li>Self-control and strong will power required</li><li>Following a protocol, a program, a diet, a mentor</li></ul>	<ul><li>Lifetime vision</li><li>More general well being</li><li>No bad or good food</li><li>Enjoyment is key</li><li>Listening to your body and his needs</li><li>Awareness and mindfulness</li><li>Plant-based diet with animal proteins in condiments</li><li>Focus on real food</li></ul>

****
Food for Thought

- ✓ Do you have experience with dieting?
- ✓ How do you approach food?
- ✓ Do you have food beliefs or food convictions?
- ✓ Are you satisfied with the way you eat?
- ✓ Have you considered seeking help for improving your family eating habits?

....
....
....
....
....
....
....
....
....
....
....
....
....
....
....
....
....
....
....
....

****

Live and Eat with Integrity

In September 2015, the day I graduated from my health coach training, I received a new visa with more rigid work restrictions. After five years spent in the U.S., I was not allowed to ask for any type of work permit. What sign was the universe trying to send me? This news was heartbreaking and very tough to accept. I thought that maybe it wasn't a good time for me to get back to work and that my family still needed me more than I thought. **Again, I tried to make the best of the situation and decided to start writing.** There was no harm in trying to write down some ideas and recipes and start creating a legacy. The health coach training helped me gain some confidence to put myself out there. I wasn't giving up and dropping everything. I was ready to share my story with the desire to empower other moms to embrace healthier eating habits.

But life rarely cooperates and goes according to plan, right? A few months later, life threw us another curveball, inviting me to take a break from writing. A new pregnancy! I was expecting a 4th daughter. But this time, conditions were different. My three other girls were older (five, seven, and eight). I was older, too, and certainly wiser, as I was ready to not repeat the mistakes I made during my third pregnancy in Baltimore. I had a solid village around me to provide all the support I needed, and I wasn't afraid to ask for help. I took care of myself in a way I had never done before: I ate very well (mostly a plant-based diet with a little bit of meat/fish twice a week), moved my body regularly (walking, swimming, dancing, and yoga), slept eight hours every night, and enjoyed journaling. I didn't force myself to do so. It just felt like the right thing to do for me. I also had the support of amazing women who helped me during labor and during the first few weeks after giving birth. What an incredible community I had around me. **I was able to walk my talk, putting into practice all I learned from my health coach training and my previous years as a full-time mom, and integrating this with my French roots.** I was living and eating in a manner which was consistent with my values, purpose, and goals. In a nutshell, I was living my life with integrity. It felt so good! When you live with integrity, you influence, inspire, and motivate others by your words and actions. Others see the positive influence that you have and want to emulate you. Isn't this what we desperately want to accomplish with our children? The beauty of integrity is that you don't have to force it or be explicit. It just comes naturally.

When it comes down to eating with integrity, in an ideal world, we must ensure that:

The food we choose to buy is safe, authentic (real food, not modified in labs), and nutritious.

The food is produced in a sustainable way with the highest ethical standards, respecting the environment and those who work in the food industry.

Of course, we do the best we can with the resources we have (time, money, skills, and knowledge). However, it is important to realize and keep in mind that everything and everyone is connected. Always trying to look for the lower prices when we buy food doesn't guarantee you the best deal in the long run. Ultimately, you pay a price for low prices.

"Food is the doorway to living well and loving well, and to fixing much of what's wrong with our world."
- Mark Hyman, American physician

****

Food for Thought

Integrity means that you have a clear sense of your moral values, and you stick to them at all costs. With that in mind:

- ✓ What is important to you? What are your core values?
- ✓ Do you feel like you live your life with integrity?
- ✓ What does it mean for you to eat food with integrity?

....
....
....
....
....
....
....
....
....

****

Food to Create Strong Communities

The first two years of raising four daughters were enlightening on so many levels. My main takeaway from this time was the **importance of being surrounded by a loving and like-minded community**. I can't emphasize enough the importance of having a supportive community around you (whether with family, church, friends...). Nobody can do everything on their own. Human nature is not meant to be individualistic. This attitude stands as well for the way we approach our health and our food choices. Food is meant to be shared. **Food is the universal bond that brings people together. Food is actually one of the things that all people, in all cultures, have in common. We celebrate and mourn over food.** While it is primarily unhealthy food that forms these bonds these days in America: sugar bomb birthday cakes, tasteless food at funerals, junk food rewards for good grades at school, mountains of sweets for Valentine's Day, Halloween, and Christmas... you get the picture. But I think it is possible to break the cycle that links junk food with those community gatherings. **There is a way to be together and healthier. We grow better together.** When you find your tribe of like-minded people sharing the same values around healthy eating habits, making changes is more manageable. You have support and accountability.

Our life in Durham brought so many positive experiences. One of the best decisions we made was to be part of a community called "Farm Church," a Christian-based church that meets on a farm and leverages the farm's resources to address food insecurity in the city. People drawn to this type of community are inclined to eat a healthier diet. Our monthly new moon potluck will be something I will forever miss! Amazing healthy food surrounded by unique and inspiring people. No greasy green bean casseroles, but instead very nourishing dishes made with care and love. We loved those monthly gatherings so much that my husband and I decided to host a weekly potluck at our apartment. Every Wednesday night, we opened our house for a mid-week break and easy way to check in and reconnect with each other. It was very informal. All were invited to attend. Bringing food wasn't required, but rather it was welcomed. I didn't make a big deal about those nights and didn't want to spend my day cooking and worrying about how many people would show up. I didn't cook anything special for the occasion, only what our family had planned to eat that night. And I just doubled or tripled the portions. It wasn't fancy in any way but rather a modest meal, consistently nutritious, and satisfying. The perfect fuel to nourish our bodies and our hearts. This mid-week gathering was so much more than filling our bellies. It was a time for empathy and generosity, a time for nourishment and communication. I can't tell you how much I got from those dinners in community. Sharing a meal together was the perfect opportunity to share our lives with each other. We got to know people more intimately. When it was time to leave, our cups were refilled, ready to shine our lights in our respective worlds. Those potlucks were such a good reminder of how we, humans, are wired. We need each other to feel whole and valuable. We need each other's gifts and stories. And what better way to do so than in front of a delicious meal. Those potlucks helped turn groups of families who lived in proximity to one another into communities of friends and neighbors. From this beloved community, I learned to never underestimate the power of food to connect with people.

****

Food for Thought

- ✓ What place does food have in your larger community (friends, church, coworkers...)?
- ✓ Do you enjoy potlucks?
- ✓ Do you have family traditions where you celebrate with food?
- ✓ Do you have a memory of an important life milestone where the care was shown with food?

****

Love for Real and Simple Food

After my fourth daughter Mathilde turned two years old, this book project came back to my mind. I felt the need to get back to writing, and finally share publicly my perspective on healthy eating, with tips and recipes I used during this very intense time of my life while raising my daughters. Of course, yet again, life had a different plan for me, and it seemed like I had to wait a little bit more before putting all my time and energy into the writing process. My husband found a position as an assistant professor in Sioux Falls, South Dakota. All those previous years of hard work were paying off, at last! In August 2019, our family did an unforgettable road trip to move to the Midwest. Another chapter of our lives was about to begin. A new adventure filled with new challenges and lessons.

During this chaotic and stressful moving period (and until the last day before leaving Durham), I did a good job maintaining regular balanced meals. I kept cooking simple and nutritious meals with what I had in my fridge and freezer. It wasn't hard because I used simple, staple, and fresh ingredients. I note this because **we can always find excuses not to cook (too tired, too busy, not the right ingredients on hand...). But if offering better food options to your family is one of your top priorities, you will take the time to do it no matter the circumstances.** It was a very challenging time for our family, so fueling our bodies with good food allowed us to handle all the ups and downs that go along with a big move.

As much as I was devastated to leave this fantastic community that we had built in Durham over the last seven years, I was also excited to discover a new state. I wanted to learn more about a different part of American culture and live in a new town. Interestingly, like my French friends, in 2010, had teased us about the junk food we would find once we moved to the U.S., our American friends from the East coast were warning us that we were moving to a Midwest meat and potato culture. They set us up to expect lots of unhealthy, hearty dishes to survive the cold. Again, I found that my first impressions about Sioux Falls were very similar to the ones I experienced when we moved to Durham. Maybe because of the concept like attracts like, I quickly found "my people" in South Dakota, bumping into lots of health-conscious people. I was so amazed by the timing of those encounters. I also think that **the mentality around food is slowly shifting in the U.S. People realize they can't keep eating like the culture promotes, using mostly convenience food.** This has a cost on their health, finances, and the environment that they are not willing to pay anymore.

In the first place, I found it challenging to make friends moving from the East Coast to the Midwest. It is definitely a different culture with different social codes. I noticed that no matter where you are in the USA, over small talk, people like to bring up two things: the weather and the food they eat! Food is always a good starter for conversations (even if you disagree with your conversation partner). And even if you don't like cooking, you usually enjoy eating and sharing food memories and stories. Food is undoubtedly what helped me make my first connections here in Sioux Falls. South Dakota is known for its fields of corn and soy. But the food scene here in Sioux Falls is pretty good. There are many good restaurants to choose from, inspiring chefs reaching out to the community by offering homemade meals or cooking classes, various programs that help you eat healthier, and the local farm-to-table movement is getting some momentum. Numerous farms and community gardens are popping up each year with a desire to share a simpler lifestyle, closer to Mother Nature. There is definitely an increased interest in local real food and home cooking. I have personally noticed that the colder weather invites me to spend more time in my kitchen, cooking more delicious soups and bread that warm my body and my soul. I have this feeling like Sioux Falls might be the perfect place to spread the word and share my passion for home cooking with simple ingredients. I don't know if it is the fact that our family can start making long term plans, but I deeply feel the drive to connect with my local community and focus primarily on the local resources available. To name a few, there are Emily Wilson, a renowned raw chef with her business, BeeLovedKitchen; Rachel DeBoer with her organization, Matriarch Movement: Health and Wellness; and Dakota Rural Action, a grassroot family agriculture and conservation group that organizes South Dakotans to protect family farmers and ranchers, natural resources, and a unique way of life. And during that same time, I was introduced to the work of amazing food writers and food activists such as Nina Planck, Alice Waters, and Barbara Kingsolver. Their dedication to promoting a simple living, using local and real ingredients is contagious. But this new chapter of my life will be for another book.

We Are What We Eat and We Eat What We Are

As I am finishing up writing this book, my French family has been living in North America for more than eleven years. It took me all this time to figure out my own relationship with healthy eating. It was very challenging to do this while immersed in a different food culture; a culture that promotes fast and cheap edible food-like substances. We never experienced food insecurity, but during the first nine years of our life abroad, our large family was living on one salary. Money was tight. We tried to be mindful about the way we spent it. After the rent, food was the second biggest expense for the household. In the long run, I know it was the right choice as it probably saved us many trips to the doctors and thousands of dollars on health bills.

Here is my thought process that slowly emerged from all those years raising four French daughters in the United States. I sum it up here with the expression "We are what we eat AND we eat what we are." Ultimately, it all comes down to that simple sentence. This double expression helps me see how central food is to our lives. Paying more attention to the food we buy and consume is the first step to a better physical, mental, and emotional health and ultimately a better world. It truly is.

We are what we eat:
The food we eat literally becomes who we are, and influences our physical, mental, and even emotional well-being. We integrate the qualities of the food we eat. **Food is information**. All calories are not created equal. The energy, composition, and spirit of the food become the energy, composition, and spirit of our whole body whether or not we are aware of it. For instance:
- eating meat from animals who were not treated well during their lifetime, and then slaughtered in cruel conditions,
- consuming food that grew using intensive farming techniques (monocropping, soil depletion, fertilizers, pesticides),
- consuming food-like items developed in labs using synthetic and artificial ingredients...

All those choices have a repercussion on our body. Our digestive system is not programmed to recognize and process this kind of information (i.e., GMOs, artificial sugars, additives). When eating processed foods, we give our body some extra work trying to make sense of it. Fake and ultra-processed foods are like a foreigner who doesn't speak our body's language, roaming the body without an itinerary, and with messages that don't translate. Choosing real food or at least foods that have been minimally processed is the way to avoid such extra work and stress on our body.

We eat what we are:
How we feel has a tremendous impact on our food choices. Have you noticed when you are rushed, stressed, angry, or sleep-deprived, you tend to eat foods that are not really good for you, relying on chips, cookies, and carbonated beverages? And on top of that, we live in a culture that promotes cheap, fast, and convenience. Our food

choices are a reflection of those traits. I am convinced that by cultivating a slower pace of life and by bringing more awareness and mindfulness around our food choices, it would make all the difference. Once you stop the autopilot mode when it comes to feeding your family, you quickly see that this is a huge systemic problem. It would be convenient to see it as an issue we can fix within our own homes and be done with it (i.e., let's make healthier food and insist our children eat it). But when you look around and realize the pervasive pressures on our children to eat bad food, it is obvious that this approach is too weak and not sufficient. Once you start making changes for your family, don't stop here. All this makes you want to become an advocate for real food accessibility and affordability.

Here is the trend I would like to see more in American households for the years to come:

Stage 1: EVALUATION OF THE CURRENT SITUATION
- ✓ Very busy family. Don't make time for meal planning and cooking
- ✓ Rely on take out and big distribution centers for grocery shopping, buying mostly prepackaged meals and snacks
- ✓ Don't really question where their food comes from
- ✓ Family mealtime is not a priority; eat in a rush, in between activities

Stage 2: AWARENESS - IS THIS SITUATION WORKING FOR MY FAMILY?
- ✓ Awareness of Stage 1
- ✓ Family not super healthy; health issues, many visits to the pediatrician and doctors, and chronic fatigue
- ✓ Weak family bonds
- ✓ Reassessment of what is important; what matters the most is the well-being of the family

Stage 3: CHANGE AT THE FAMILY LEVEL
- ✓ Need to change collective eating habits as a family
- ✓ Become more mindful about food choices
- ✓ Focus on simple meals made with real food
- ✓ Grocery shopping at the same location as before but limit shopping experience to the fresh sections
- ✓ That's where a Holistic Health Coach, like myself, can help. (Keep reading through the book. You are getting close to the juicy content!)

Stage 4: CHANGE AT THE SOCIETY LEVEL
- ✓ Better understanding that the food we choose to buy is a political act

- ✓ Everything and everyone are interconnected, interdependent, and interrelated: how we feed ourselves, how we care for neighbors and workers, and how we treat the natural resources of the planet
- ✓ We all have a part in this economy. As a consumer, you may be at the end of the chain but how you spend your money tells small producers, and bigger food corporations what you want or don't want. Your decisions matter

I have a dream, an ideal vision of how feeding our families and ourselves could look like in the future. It could be easy. It could be simple. Throughout the seasons and the stages of our lives, we would listen to our bodies and choose the right food and the right portions, relying on our internal wisdom rather than an external source of knowledge. We would stick with real and simple foods, using mostly a short chain food supply and supporting the local economy. We would all have the basic cooking skills and techniques to create quick and easy homemade meals. There would be no commercials trying to confuse us and convince us to buy fake foods. We wouldn't need to counterbalance our consumption of junk food with expensive food supplements and doctor's appointments. We would live in a world where there are no fad diets or food deprivation. We would simply eat close to what Mother Nature has to offer in her simplest way, mostly fruits and veggies, avoiding ultra-processed foods. We would become more comfortable with our discomfort and not use food as a buffer to deal with our emotions. As parents, we would intrinsically know how to make the best decisions around planning, shopping, cooking, and eating for our families. Our children would naturally model their eating behaviors from what they observe from us. They would be taught how to cook and the importance of eating well at an early age. In a nutshell, feeding ourselves and our families would be a simple and joyful task. We would all consider food no more or no less than it is: Fueling our bodies with good energy and nutrients AND enjoying it without seeing it as a burden or a reward.

Now, dear reader, I can already hear you say "Sandrine, this vision seems too good to be true. This world is out of reach and will stay as you described it: a dream."

I get it and truly understand where you are coming from with this concern. That's why in the next section of this book, we will take the time to dive into all the common concerns and questions you might have around changing your family eating habits. Every change starts with one small step. Don't get discouraged. Stay hopeful.

PART THREE:
Common Questions and Concerns
About Making
Food Habits Changes

"I don't like to give advice. I like to give people information because everyone's life is different, and everyone's journey is different."
- Dolly Parton, American singer and songwriter

Why Bother with Home Cooking?

"Inevitably, the manufacturers of processed food argue that they have allowed us to become the people we want to be, fast and busy, no longer slaves to the stove. But in their hands, the salt, sugar, and fat they have used to propel this social transformation are not nutrients as much as they are weapons - weapons they deploy, certainly, to defeat their competitors but also to keep us coming back for more."

- Michael Moss, author of Salt, Sugar, Fat

While we have never stopped eating, many of us have stopped cooking. It makes sense to ask ourselves why we should do more home cooking. It is such a great question! After all, we live in the 21st century. Why spend time cooking when we could do so many other things? Plus, there are myriads of food businesses willing to help in that domain (i.e., meal planners, food delivery services, take out). The American food industry is also reinforcing the message that taking the time to cook at home is not very valuable and trendy (hello frozen and prepackaged meals). It seems like the less time you spend in the kitchen, the better.

With that background, this comes as no surprise that home cooking isn't very appealing and prevalent in the U.S. I am definitely biased with my French roots because the love of food is in my DNA. I don't necessarily enjoy cooking but because my desire to eat good food is so strong, I am making most of our meals at home. Also, I often think about my four children and how I want them to have the basic skills in the kitchen to be independent and resourceful when they leave the house. It is very important to me to transmit this love for good food at an early age. Learning to cook simple meals is not has-been. It is a very valuable lifetime skill that serves all people. There is also some pride around being able to feed you and your family nourishing meals. We can't expect junk food and fast-food companies to promote healthy diets and active lifestyles when they are the antithesis of those things.

There is a huge difference between eating at home and cooking at home. If you grew up with convenience food being your norm, you may be lacking some basic food education and cooking skills. Maybe reheating a frozen industrial pre-made meal in the microwave is all you know about "cooking at home." And that is ok. There is a whole spectrum when we talk about home cooking, with various levels of expertise. Just know where you are currently and start from there.

Zero home cooking	You don't like cooking at all and prefer eating out as much as you can. You have zero cooking skills.	
Eat at home, but don't really cook	Take out and meals deliveries are the norm for your family. You buy mostly frozen pre-made meals that you will reheat at home. You have the resources to hire a private chef.	
Cook at home	**Out of the Box Cook** You cook at home with some fresh vegetables but mostly using shortcuts from the food industry (hello cake mix, mac and cheese box, frozen meals, frozen meats and vegetables). Or you have the possibility to use meal-kit companies that deliver everything you need to cook a meal.	
	In Between Category You use a combination of DIY projects from scratch using natural ingredients with some shortcuts from store-bought processed foods.	
	Only Real Food Cook You buy fresh produce at the store and cook at home. You master some useful cooking skills. You are mindful about where the food comes from and try to eat local.	
	The Ultimate Home Cook You cook every single thing from scratch. You have your own garden, chicken coop and there is a hunter in the family! You do everything from scratch. Definitely not the majority of people nowadays. But let's remember that our ancestors, just a few generations ago, were in that category.	

****

Invitation to Action

- ✓ What kind of home cook are you?
- ✓ What are your aspirations in the kitchen?
- ✓ Reading suggestion: *We Are What We Eat: A Slow Food Manifesto* by Alice Waters.

....
....
....
....
....
....
....
....
....
....
....
....
....
....
....
....
....

****

With the fast-paced life most of us are experiencing and the stress associated with this lifestyle, how on earth do I dare encourage you to do more home cooking? It may sound old-fashioned and time-consuming, but I truly believe that it is one of the best things you can do for the health of your whole family. When you cook at home, you are in complete control of the ingredients and how you are using them. You know exactly what you are putting in your body. And you can flavor the food you cook the way it pleases you and your family most.

I Don't Have Time to Cook

"Time is what we want most, but what we use worst."
-William Penn, English Quaker leader

I totally understand and acknowledge this concern. For many of us, time feels like a scarce resource. Life seems to move faster than ever. We are in a constant state of struggling to keep up. With our never-ending to-do list, it is like multitasking has become a skill to master. We want to feel this illusion that we have it all, juggling our jobs and families, commitments with community organizations, staying connected with friends, and maintaining households. The list goes on and on. At the end of the day, we don't even feel happy about ourselves for accomplishing what we did, already thinking about what needs to be done the next day. Does this sound all too familiar? One important thing that we tend to forget is that **when we say yes to something, it means we say no to something else**. For instance, saying yes to volunteering on a committee we don't love also implies that we say no to time with family.

Time is our most precious resource. It is the one thing in life that we can't get more of. Every person has the same amount to leverage: 24 hours a day. Why do some people get way more done than others? For the middle class in America, it is a question of time management and setting up priorities. Time management is not about learning how to do things faster or cramming more stuff into our days. It is choosing where and how to spend our time. As Marie Forleo said beautifully, "If it is important enough, you will make the time. If it is not, you will make an excuse." It might be interesting to pause for a minute and think about how you spend your time in a day. We often think that we don't have control over how our daily schedule unfold, but we really do. The struggle for most people is understanding what a priority is and what it isn't. How do we prioritize when we feel like everything is important? Are you choosing to spend your time being busy, or are you choosing to focus your day on what matters most? What are your priorities, and how do you honor them during your days?

Treat your time with respect. Value it and it will serve you. If having a healthier lifestyle is <u>really</u> on your priority list, you will find a way to carve some time to make it happen. Simply put, be very clear with your intentions (the why behind your actions) and always keep them in mind (write them down, make them visible, share them with a friend who can keep you accountable). Let's be honest here: you probably already know that cooking for your family will take more time than throwing a frozen pizza in the oven. But deciding to prioritize your health is so worth the investment! Change your perspective. See the time you spend cooking in your kitchen as an excellent opportunity to invest in your health. By doing so, you will spend less time and money at the doctor's office later. Better to pay the grocer than the doctor!

Cooking can be an enjoyable and rewarding activity without being too time-consuming. Hence, the purpose of this book. I wrote it to support you on this journey. There are strategies to get healthy homemade meals ready every night without spending tons of time in the kitchen. The Guidelines section (Part 4) of the book will help you get started.

Lastly, there is a cultural aspect regarding the time we spend cooking and eating. For instance, in cultures with a long culinary history (as in France or Japan), preparing wholesome foods is typical and expected. They prepare slowly and eat slowly. They don't expect meals to be ready immediately and they savor their meals.

The U.S. is a relatively new country of mixed heritage. There is not a unifying anchor around food.

****

Invitation to Action

"How we spend our days is, of course, how we spend our lives."
-Annie Dillard, America author

No matter where you think your priorities are, where you devote your time is what you're choosing to make a priority in your life. Have you already used a time log? It is a straightforward yet eye-opening tool to have a better sense of where you devote your attention. Start tracking with honesty every moment of your days for a couple of weeks by 15-min, 30-min, or 1-hour increments so you can find out if your perception of how you are spending your time is matched up with reality. You can do this the old-fashioned way using a piece of paper and a pen or go digital using time tracking apps. You can also start monitoring your screen time on your phone and look at the apps you are spending more time on.

****

I Don't Have Any Help

"One of the biggest defects in life is the inability to ask for help."
-Robert Kiyosaki, American businessman and author

This is a really important factor and a common concern for many of you. I see more and more single parents trying so hard to do it all because they don't have any other options. They wear way too many hats (i.e., child rearing, housekeeping, professional career, parents' caregiver). To some extent, nuclear families deal with the same issue. Our current society tends to promote isolation and individualism, and this sets us up for failure. The demands of working and parenting in the 21st century feels impossible to fulfill. The surge of COVID-19 has made things even worse in that regard. Parents have been asked an impossible task. Compared to a few generations ago, we have lost a fair amount of immediate support from family and connections. We are not supposed to do everything on our own, plus with the expectation of doing it perfectly. **We just can't do it all and are not meant to do it all**. We are social creatures who need the support of a community to survive and thrive.

So, in the context of changing eating habits, I invite you to explore the following suggestions to get help.

First of all, ask yourself about the changes you want to make. Set your intentions and write down your vision. Be very specific and take in account your personal situation. Whether you are a single parent, parenting an infant, toddler or teenager, with family and friends close by to help or not, you won't all have the same answers. The more specific you can be, the easier it is to then communicate your ideas to family and friends and seek appropriate help and support.

Ask for help from your partner. Make an assessment about your current situation. See what is working and what is not. Share your ideas. If your partner doesn't want to cook, he/she still can help with planning, doing the groceries, chopping vegetables, or doing the dishes.

If your kids are old enough, organize a family meeting and communicate your intentions. Again, be clear and specific about what changes you would like to make. Include them in the conversation, solicit their opinions, ask them how they could contribute. For instance, you can put the kids in charge of dish duty or assign your teenager to make dinner one night a week.

When we want to make some changes in our lives (no matter the domain), accountability is key. Could you find a friend who would also be interested in changing their family eating habits? Having a reliable partner to discuss your struggles or share your successes is an invaluable help. Think about your village. Do you have any friends or acquaintances who love to cook? Would they be willing to share some cooking skills and tips with you? Maybe share one or two easy fool-proof recipes?

You could partner with another family with whom you feel close to and share meals or recipes. Cooking meals together or doubling a recipe so you can share and exchange meals works very well for some people. If you have young kids at home, you can organize a playdate while the parents gather to cook. There are probably families in your neighborhood who would love to make new connections and learn how to cook some new dishes. You have nothing to lose by asking. It is worth trying!

If your food budget is not too tight, you might find it helpful to use some external food services. There are so many companies out there nowadays offering different types of meal planning and meal delivery support:

Meal Planning Services:
- **The Fresh 20**: Shop, Prep and Cook 5 healthy dinners using just 20 fresh ingredients, with no waste! This company provides easy, unprocessed meal plans created by chef, and approved by registered dieticians. Dinner is simple to cook, and delicious.
- **Plan to Eat:** This company has been around for 10 years now. They help you collect your own recipes that fit your lifestyle, create a customized meal plan to accommodate your schedule, then go to the store with a list organized the way you like to shop.
- **Once a Month Meals**: This company gives you everything you need to shop, prep and cook the bulk of your monthly meals in just one day — and freeze those meals for when you want to eat them.

Meal Delivery Kits:
- **Hello Fresh**: This meal-kit company is based in Berlin, Germany. It is the largest meal-kit provider in the United States. You get everything you need to cook delicious meals delivered to your door. Easy-to-follow recipes with clear nutritional info, high-quality ingredients sourced straight from the farm. convenient meal kits that fit perfectly in the fridge
- **Blue Apron**: This company is committed to provide a better food system by: partnering with farmers to raise the highest-quality ingredient, creating a distribution system that delivers ingredients at a better value , investing in the things that matter most—our environment and our communities
- **Home Chefs**: It is a Chicago, Illinois-based meal kit and food delivery company that delivers pre-portioned ingredients and recipes to subscribers weekly in

the United States. You are clearly not the only American family wanting to make some eating habits changes. I am amazed by the number of online resources available nowadays. Here are a few I found interesting in 2022.

- **The Family Dinner Project** : It is a nonprofit initiative started in 2010. This organization sees family dinner as an opportunity for family members to connect with each other through food, fun and conversation about things that matter.

Online Cooking Classes:

- **Ktichn Cooking School:** Sign up any time to receive 20 lessons daily to help you on the journey of becoming the cook you've always wanted to be.
- **ToTaste:** It is a culinary nutrition consulting company that provides culinary nutrition experiences through cooking demonstrations, nutrition talks, health fair booths, hands on cooking classes, recipe development, curriculum development, and more.

****

Invitation to Action

✓ Have a conversation with your partner so you can start sharing more of the load of feeding the family.
✓ Name 3 persons you can ask for help to change your eating habits.
✓ Set up a conversation with them and come up with an action plan.

....
....
....
....
....
....

****

I Am Too Tired

"Rest and self-care are so important. When you take time to replenish your spirit, it allows you to serve others from the overflow. You cannot serve from an empty vessel."
– Eleanor Brown, American novelist

"The deeper we are into adulthood, the more we have to navigate the needs of others as well as our own."
- Erica Layne, Blogger (thelifeonpurposemovement.com) and Certified Life Coach

Motherhood is simultaneously the toughest yet most rewarding job in the world. Contrary to all the other "regular" paying jobs out there, you can't really take a break from this one. You can't wake up one morning and simply decide not to take care of your children or skip out on feeding them.

The first years of motherhood are probably the period in life when we need the most support and the most amount of self-compassion. Yet, we often make a mistake to give more than we can, sometimes feeling completely depleted. In the end, we have nothing left to offer except resentment and grumpiness. I learned this lesson the hard way, raising four daughters in a foreign country without asking for help initially and beating myself up for things I didn't have time to accomplish during the day.
I was so harsh on myself. This is probably the biggest lesson I have learned in my life so far: if I want to be a caring and loving mom, I have to take care of myself first. It

has to be my priority if I want everything else to fall into place (cooking good meals for my family included). Taking good care of yourself is not selfish because it is the fuel that makes all other care and all other activities possible. Unfortunately, these days, self-care is becoming a buzzword. It has turned into a luxury instead of necessary daily practice. When we think of self-care, we often think bubble bath, pedicure, massage, or a night out. Although these things are lovely to do and could be part of your self-care routine, we should not consider self-care as a one-time deal. Randi Kay, an expert on helping women create effective seasonal healing practices, defines **self-care as a practice of tuning in to our true needs, listening, and acting accordingly.** Tuning in instead of tuning out.

It will look different to everyone. Choose what you would enjoy, but it is essential to find a DAILY practice. So please, before diving into meal planning and cooking, get away from the Superwoman syndrome and take the time to think about your self-care situation first. Self-care is an agreement with yourself. You don't need permission from someone else to do things for yourself. I know how hard it is to shift our perspective around self-care. We haven't been taught and are not used to putting ourselves first. And if we do so, it feels selfish. Self-care is hard to do because it all comes down to self-worth and self-love.

I often remind myself that the best gift I can give to my children is my own happiness. Imagine for one minute raising the next generation of human beings with awareness around self-care. Your daughter would see how you made sure your needs were a priority, so when she becomes a mom, it's natural for her to take care of herself, too. Your son would see you voice your needs as a mom and a woman and so he can empower the same culture for women in his life in the future.

That being said, I want to emphasize how difficult it is to implement self-care practices when we have small children. With this season of life now behind me, I keep wondering if I would have been able to take better care of myself knowing what I know

now. Whatever your situation is, learn to ask for help and surround yourself with friends who are willing to support you. Here are some ideas of simple self-care practices for a healthy mind, body, and soul:

First, and probably most importantly: **Sleep**. Nothing else except breathing and drinking water is immediately vital to our well-being as sleep. Sleep doesn't have a good reputation. Thinking that we spend close to a third of our life sleeping feels like a waste of time for many. But if you don't get the right amount of sleep, your time spent awake will be a waste, too. Sleep allows your body and your brain to have a break from all the information processed during the day. Sleep quite literally renews your body and mind. When you are sleep deprived, your brain can't function properly, affecting your cognitive abilities and emotional state. You tend to compensate with food, overeating, and leaning on not-so-healthy-high-energy food for a quick fix. Try as much as you can to have at least 7 to 8 hours of sleep every night.

Breathing is the one movement we do more than any other. It becomes so natural that we don't even think about it. Taking the time to focus on our breath, even for just a couple of minutes every day, can have excellent results on our health. **Reconnect with your body, your lifetime companion**. Learn how to tune in and see what your body pain is telling you. The pain you are experiencing is not a punishment but a simple signal from your body telling you to slow down and pay attention. Something needs to be addressed.

Honor your rhythms and energy levels. For years, I have felt bad about myself because I didn't seem to have constant energy. But then, thanks to Kate Northrup, author of Do Less: A Revolutionary Approach to Time and Energy Management for Ambitious Women, I came to understand that human beings are cyclical. Women cycle on a 28-day rotation while men cycle on a 24-hour rotation. Men go through all the phases in a day, while women go through them in a month. The way the world is set up doesn't reflect the way that women's bodies are wired but instead celebrates the masculine cycle. When I started paying more attention to my cycle and the different phases I was going through, it was a total game changer! During our reproductive years, we cycle on a roughly 28-day rotation with four distinct phases. Each phase has its own unique gifts and opportunities if we pay attention to them. Your body has innately so much power and wisdom.

Here's a quick cheat-sheet for you:

• Week 1 = Menstrual phase
 	
  REST AND REFLECT
 	
• Around day 1-6 of your menstrual cycle when you're bleeding.
• Inner Winter
	• Week 2 = Follicular phase
	
	  PLAN AND INITIATE
	
	• Around day 7-13 when you're in the pre-ovulation phase.
	• Inner Spring

• Week 3 = Ovulation phase
 	
  CONNECT AND BE VISIBLE
 	
• Around day 14-21 during your ovulation phase.
• Inner Summer
	• Week 4 = Luteal phase
	
	  FOCUS AND COMPLETE
	
	• Around day 22-29 during your luteal phase
	• Inner Fall

Have a morning or evening routine. Choose something that lights you up. It could be journaling, prayers, meditation, morning affirmations, exercising, walking, a quiet time before the kids wake up, or eating a healthy breakfast...

Mindfulness. Take some daily time to step back and tune in, reflecting, sitting still, paying attention to your body and your feelings. It doesn't have to be long. Just two minutes before going to bed to review your day can be enough. You become more aware of how you are living your life and what would need to be changed.

Cultivate gratitude. Take a few minutes every day to see the beauty all around you. There are good things no matter how many hard challenges you are facing.

Have a self-date. Spend an hour alone doing something that nourishes you and brings you joy. It could be practicing a hobby, reading, visiting a museum or gallery, gardening, taking a relaxing bath, or doing nothing! Enjoy your own company. Honor this time with yourself and treat it like if you were scheduling an appointment with a client. Mark it on your calendar and make it count.

Spend time outside whatever the weather is. Go for a run or a walk, even if it is just for a few minutes. Use different itineraries and pay attention to what is around you. You can also try cloud-watching: lie on your back, relax, and watch the sky. My kids love to do that with me! In 2019, our family moved from North Carolina to South Dakota. Despite the contrast of temperatures, I still made a point to go outside every day. And the big open sky makes our sky watching experience even more interesting. There is so much wisdom and power in nature. I like this mantra in that regard: "Doctor cares, Nature cures."

Set up a time to unplug for a couple of hours or even longer if you can. Switch your devices to airplane mode and free yourself from the constant "binges" of social media and email. Those digital distractions take you away from your real life and your goals.

Put on your favorite upbeat record and dance. I love doing that with my daughters for 5 minutes. We call it "fou-fou time" (crazy time). Music and/or movement are powerful tools to help you disconnect with your day-to-day life and get back to your body.

Have a good laugh! It will help you revitalize yourself and see things in a more positive way. If you find it hard to laugh, start by putting a smile on your face (even if it may feel forced), and you'll find that the world really does smile back at you and with you. Give it a try. You will be amazed by the results.

Choose carefully who you spend your time with. Hang out with people who emit enthusiasm and positivity, and not with those whose pessimism and negativity robs your energy. Being surrounded by people and especially other women who inspire you makes a huge difference.

Read inspirational quotes or biographies of people you admire. Or watch some interviews with inspiring individuals. It works all the time for me when I feel stuck or too negative.

And the list goes on, but you get the idea. Your brain and body are all you have. Your work, your family, and your friends all rely on your well-being. Everything depends on your vitality and health.

I like how Nicholas Bate refers to this daily checking in as "**Taking your MEDS.**"
- **M**indfulness (what you think)
- **E**xercise (breathing and movement)
- **D**iet (what you eat)
- **S**leep

So, tell me, have you been **"Taking your MEDS"** daily these days?

****

Invitation to Action

- ✓ Take the time to ask yourself those questions:
- ✓ What is your personal definition of self-care?
- ✓ What does your current self-care practice look like?

✓ What brings you joy? What makes you miserable?

....
....
....
....
....
....
....
....
....
....
....
....
....
....
....
....
....
....
....
....

Think about ways you could add more daily things that add joy to your life and do fewer things that don't fulfill you. At the end, you always have the choice.

Choose one or two activities (from listed above, or some of your own) that make you feel good and could be implemented in your daily life. Mark them down on your agenda. Honor them and make them count as if it was a professional appointment. And do it DAILY. Eventually, I would love you to feel like those self-care moments are an essential part of your day. You wouldn't even question them. They become automatic, like brushing your teeth. Remember self-care practice comes down to self-worth. And let me tell you, without a doubt, that you are worth it. No conditions required.

I'm Too Overwhelmed

"The more ingredients in a packaged food, the more highly processed it probably is."

- Michael Pollan, American author, and journalist

Oh, I hear you, mama! It drives me crazy! Our supermarkets are filled with thousands of items. Unfortunately, most of them are processed, filled with sugar, fat, and additives. I won't even dare to call it food. The food industry is doing an amazing job paying millions of dollars in marketing and research, so we get more addicted to their products. We shouldn't feel bad about ourselves because we don't know how to make good choices around food. This confusion is created and maintained so we keep buying products that are not so good for us.

And unfortunately, even if we stay away from those packaged items, we are still confused about what we are supposed to eat. We don't really get help from top nutrition experts. They themselves have to deal with lots of contradictory information. Some of them will swear by a strict plant-based diet, as for others it will be a paleo, gluten-free, or vegan diet, etc. You can find a guru for each diet praising that they found THE right way to eat. Nutrition is such a bizarre science. It is the only field where people can scientifically prove opposing theories and still be right. Ugh... So, how do we know what is best to do? I have good news and bad news for you.

The good news is that you can stop the confusion by simply remembering what real food is. Eat mostly things that come from the ground or found in nature. The less processed, the better. It is important to keep in mind what food is and is not. Today, we live in a world of convenience food. It is commercially prepared for ease of consumption. This type of food has been "created" (not harvested) to make it more appealing to the consumer, but unfortunately, it is not nutritious. It might save you time but certainly not money and wellbeing. I would even go further saying that it is depleting us and making us sick. Would you trade your health for convenience? Is it really worth it in the long run?

Let's play a little game of guessing. What "food" is it?

Ingredients: Enriched flour (wheat flour, niacin, reduced iron, vitamin B1 [thiamin mononitrate], vitamin B2 [riboflavin], folic acid), corn syrup, high fructose corn syrup, sugar, soybean, palm oil (with TBQH for freshness), dextrose, contains two percent or less of wheat starch, glycerin, cracker meal, salt, dried strawberries, dried pears, dried apples, leavening (baking soda, sodium acid pyrophosphate, monocalcium phosphate), citric acid, milled corn, gelatin, malic acid, soybean oil, modified corn starch, xantham gum, color added, soy lecithin, modified wheat starch, red 40, turmeric for color, carmine color, vitamin A palmitate, niacinamide, reduced iron, yellow 6, vitamin B6 (pyridoxine hydrochloride), natural and artificial flavor, vitamin B2 (riboflavin), vitamin B1 (thiamin hydrochloride), blue 1.	Ingredients: carrot
Answer: pop tart	Answer: carrot

Simplicity and common sense are my mottos. When you feel lost and don't know what to buy and what to eat, this easy to remember acronym is a good reminder. It sums it up pretty well. Eat less CRAP and eat more real FOOD.

Less CRAP	More Real FOOD
C– carbonated drinks **R**– refined sugar **A**– artificial sweeteners and colors **P**– processed foods	**F**– fruits and veggies **O**–organic proteins **O**– omega 3 fatty acids **D**– drink water Food that comes directly from Mother Earth

Do not let terms like zero trans- fat, low sodium, 100% natural, or sugar-free, fool you into thinking that processed food is healthy. The only way to know what is really in your food is to read the ingredient labels. Or even better, buy food that is the closest to its natural state (in that case, no need for labels). Buy food that your grandmother and great-grandmother would recognize and eat.

"A guide to safer eating in a poisoned world might well be: avoid those foods that are imperishable. Eat only those foods that spoil, or rot or decay but eat them before they do."
-Helen Nearing, author of *Simple Food for a Good Life*

The bad news is that you have to figure out by yourself what real food works best for you. It is the concept of bio-individuality. We are all different. Personal differences in anatomy, metabolism, body composition, and cell structure all influence our overall health and the food that makes us feel our best. There is no one-size-fits-all diet. Each person is a unique individual with personalized nutritional needs. It is our responsibility for each of us to find the right food that will optimize our health. We won't find the answer in textbooks, cookbooks, or seminars from nutrition experts. We have to do the work and start questioning our eating habits. We have to experiment and try for ourselves, paying attention to how we feel after we eat something.

For optimal health, we should focus on eating real whole foods such as vegetables, fruits, legumes, beans, whole grains, nuts, and seeds. Forget about processed packaged foods. For more controversial food such as dairy, gluten, meat, and fish, I feel like it is more of a personal choice depending on how much your body needs and how it tolerates those foods. Other factors include your personal values around the economy and the environment. It really is simple, but we live in a culture that keeps us confused.

****

Invitation to Action

- ✓ Read the book *In Defense of Food* by Michael Pollan.
- ✓ Next time you go to a grocery store, I challenge you to buy only real foods. Skip the aisles at the center of the store and shop at the periphery where the fresh produce and other fresh departments are located. If you have to buy packaged foods, take the time to read the labels. If there are ingredients listed that you can't find in nature, leave it on the shelf and choose a better option that fits your budget.

****

It is Too Expensive

"Eating healthy is expensive. Not eating healthy is expensive. One dents your pocket. The other dents your health"
– Mokokoma Mokhonoana, philosopher, social critic, graphic designer

Let's break the myth once and for all that eating healthy (whatever that might mean to you) is automatically super-pricey. If you tried to replace regular package foods for healthier versions, you probably noticed that your food budget blew up. And on top of that, those supposed healthier versions are not. Just read the labels. When you buy prepared or packaged food (organic or not), you are paying an extra convenience fee. Below are a few thoughts about eating on a budget.

Make sure to always have these **pantry basic ingredients** that are fairly inexpensive and nourishing: beans, lentils, sweet potatoes, potatoes, frozen vegetables, cabbage, whole carrots, hummus, rice, eggs, and a whole chicken. I like to call them cheap real food.

Try to buy in bulk. Most of the time, items in bulk are cheaper per pound, and you can buy the exact quantity you need. We buy all our oats, nuts, seeds, beans, lentils, dried herbs, and most of our flour in bulk. Bulk aisles are prevalent in health food stores but also more and more present in some regular grocery stores. Online stores are also good options.

You don't need to buy everything organic. What really matters is how the food was grown. Some smaller farms use all organic practices but haven't gone through the full organic certification process yet because it can be expensive for a small business. Get to know your local farms, take the time to ask about the farm's practices at the farmer's market. When shopping at traditional grocery stores, I use the Environmental Working Group's (EWG) Shopper's Guide to Pesticides in Produce™ to choose which produce items I'll buy organic. This Dirty Dozen and Clean 15 list are updated annually and ranks pesticide contamination on forty-eight popular fruits and vegetables.

Here are their lists for 2022:

THE DIRTY DOZEN Buy these organic whenever possible	THE CLEAN 15 These are ok to buy conventional (not organic)
1. Strawberries 2. Spinach 3. Kale 4. Nectarines 5. Apples 6. Grapes 7. Bell / hot peppers 8. cherries 9. Peaches 10. Pears 11. Celery 12. tomatoes	1. Avocados 2. Sweet Corn 3. Pineapple 4. Onions 5. Papayas 6. Sweet peas (frozen) 7. Asparagus 8. Honeydew melon 9. Kiwi 10. Cabbage 11. Mushroom 12. Cantaloupe 13. Mangoes 14. Watermelon 15. Sweet potatoes

Quick shopping tip: PLU codes are **4- or 5-digit numbers that appear on a small sticker applied to the individual piece of fresh produce**. on the quality of the item.

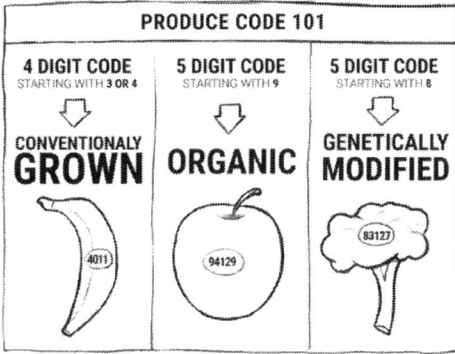

Try to buy the best food quality you can afford.

Eat with the seasons and preferably choose local. When you eat this way, it's better for your health since foods that are grown and consumed during their appropriate seasons are more nutritionally dense; it's better for the environment because there is a fuel emission cost for long travel food, and it's cheaper since fruits and vegetables in season are abundant thus available at a lower price. If going to the farmer's market, or meeting the local farmers is too much for you right now (or too much of a stretch to your current grocery habits), start by buying fresh fruits and vegetables at your routine grocery store.

Reduce your meat consumption. Meat can be very expensive, especially when it is humanely raised. Try to stretch your ground meat dishes using lentils or adding vegetables such as mushrooms and carrots. Meat has never been the center of our meal. We like to use it as more of a side dish or condiment.

Skip flavored beverages. They can add up pretty fast. It will be good for your wallet and your health, too. There are easy ways to make your own naturally flavored water if you are not a fan of plain water. You can use a combination of fresh fruits and herbs and add them to your water (strawberry/lemon/basil - watermelon/mint - cucumber/lime/mint...)

Buy frozen vegetables and fruits. These are fairly inexpensive yet very nutritious because they are picked and frozen at their peak of freshness, which beats the canned alternative and sometimes even the fresh produce that are off-season. Frozen berries are a perfect addition to yogurt or cereal. Also, frozen vegetables blends are convenient for a quick and easy stir-fry or fried rice dish.

Another major key to saving money is **making the most of the food you buy and not letting it go to waste**. How many times did you have to throw away food that you bought a few days ago because you just forgot about it? You know, those sad green onions or bags of lettuce you find wilted and soupy at the bottom of your refrigerator. You could save hundreds of dollars every year if you try to be more mindful of the food you already have in your house.

If you need another argument or some more inspiration, my friend Aurelie Barrial has taken up the challenge to cook healthy meals on a budget. In her book, Cooking for $1, she proves that you can eat well without breaking the bank. She details all the prices and demonstrates that you can eat delicious home-cooked meals under $1 (by portion).

****

Invitation to Action

- ✓ Do you know how much you spend on groceries every week? If you have no idea, it might be helpful to start paying attention to your expenses. Be curious.
- ✓ Similar to logging your time, find a system to keep track of your food expenses for one or two months (i.e., groceries, snacks, drive-thru coffee, eating out, take-out). Every small food expense counts.

****

I Don't Want to Remove Foods from My Diet

"There is no diet that will do what healthy eating does."
-Unknown

I have noticed that particularly in the U.S, people have strong, black-and-white opinions about food. There are bad foods we should avoid as much as possible and good foods we should consume in a great amount. There is definitely a trend for going sugar-free, gluten-free, wheat-free, and/or dairy-free. But in my opinion, there is no need to remove all gluten, sugar, and dairy from your diet. **You don't need to be extreme in your food choices and totally remove a food group from your diet** unless you have any severe food allergies or symptoms showing that you would do better without them. In some cases, when people reach such an unhealthy state threatening their lives, it might be necessary to make drastic changes for a short period of time (we call it an elimination diet). BUT it is not sustainable. This is the dichotomy between diet and lifestyle. As soon as you cut out some food groups from your eating pattern, you are on a diet/restriction mode. Your body won't like it and will freak out.

I think it all comes down to a question of moderation, self-reflection, and quality of food. The problem with gluten, dairy, and sugar is that it shouldn't be the foundation of our diet and consumed in such a great amount, which is sadly the case today in the U.S. Whereas if the base of your diet is from foods that are the closest to nature (vegetables, fruits, whole grains, nuts, seeds, beans, lentils, and water), there is not much room left for controversial foods.

You also need to pay attention to how you feel after you eat. Do you feel energized or lethargic and ready for a nap after eating a bagel with cream cheese or a doughnut? Would you feel the same way if you ate a mixed salad filled with lean protein, vegetables, and whole grains? Be aware of the signs your body is sending you after you eat something. That is the best indicator to see if your food choices are the best for you and your body type.

Select good quality foods. This is essential, especially with the food you think you should avoid (i.e., sugar, dairy, flour, oil). Buy the best quality you can afford and avoid packaged foods with ingredients you can't even pronounce.

If you really listen to your body and pay attention to the messages it is sending you, you'll begin to feel foods are the right fuel to give your body the energy you need to get through your day and which foods do not. Symptoms such as skin problems, digestive issues, bloating, gas, fatigue, and lack of concentration are often signs of overconsumption of those foods. That being said, as a French woman, it would be very hard for me to give up on a good slice of homemade fresh baked bread, a delicious pastry, or good quality cheese! I am just mindful of the choices I make, especially around this type of food. And one rule of thumb is that they are not the base of any of the meals I have. My base is a whole food, plant-based diet.

I personally don't eat much dairy because my stomach doesn't like it. I will use whole milk and heavy cream to bake or cook things at home, and in that case, I can tolerate it in a moderate amount. We use flour quite often as I bake a lot of bread. I can find good quality at various grocery stores or co-op. The bulk section is often a great place to find fresh and local flours. And I also always have some form of sugar in my pantry. I try to go for the most natural and the least refined sources of sugar such as fruit, coconut sugar, honey, maple syrup, and dried fruits. I also have cane sugar that is refined. If I do buy canned or packaged food, I make sure to read the labels beforehand and check the amount of added sugar or salt. The solution I found for my family about eating these "evil food groups" is to make homemade treats. Doing so, I know all the ingredients I use, plus I have some control over the amount of sugar used. I actually found it a little ironic that most of my repertoire of French recipes calls for flour, butter, sugar, and eggs. You just change the proportion of each ingredient and you get all sorts of delicious traditional French food: quiche, bread, crêpes, flan, French toast, crumble, pie dough, crème pâtissière (vanilla custard), Île flottante (floating island), and béchamel (white sauce). If I had to cut gluten and dairy from my diet, I would have had to say good-bye to all the French staple foods!

****

Invitation to Action

- ✓ I feel like a broken record but starting to bring your day-to-day food choices to your awareness is a crucial step towards a healthier lifestyle. And the best way to do this is by using a food journal where you track down every bite of food you consume. Be honest with yourself: nibbling while preparing dinner or eating a bag of chips because we had a rough day all count.
- ✓ Read the book *How to Eat - All Your Food and Diet Questions Answered* by Mark Bittman and David L. Katz, MD. A question-answer format kind of book with a conversational style that will help you bring back some common sense to your food choices.

****

I Am Not a Good Example for My Kids

*"Kids are like a mirror, what they see and hear, they do.
Be a good reflection for them."*
– Kevin Heath, former Australian football player

Your own relationship with food is indeed an important concern, especially when you have a family to feed. The good news is that often times, as we become parents, we feel the drive to give our children the best start in life and it often includes making better food choices. For instance, when you can, you are willing to pay extra dollars to buy food with no pesticides or added sugar. I think our relationship with food is the first thing we need to pay attention to when we want to change our family eating habits because it can have an impact on two different levels:

On a practical level, you may be the main cook in the family. So, it can definitely be challenging to cook food that you don't like or don't know how to cook for the sake of expanding your little ones' taste buds. Generally, you tend to buy food and prepare meals that you enjoy eating yourself.

On an emotional level, like it or not, you are a role model for your children, and they will pick up pretty quickly (and replicate) your eating habits. It is also important to separate any of your own emotional baggage with food with your child's diet. It can become a pernicious way to plant the seed for creating an unhealthy relationship with food. It is important to be aware of your own anxieties around your child's eating. Children can sense when we are worried or frustrated about their eating and that can feel like pressure to them. And it surely doesn't help them eat better.

The first thing to do is to ask yourself some important questions. Try to go through all the thoughts, beliefs, rules, principles, and values you have around food and eating habits. Write them down, scan them, and ask yourself if they are serving you. If you don't like your answers, take the time to write down what it would be like for you to have a good relationship with food.

It might seem difficult to believe that our tastes and eating habits are not fixed and can be changeable (particularly those so bound up with memories of family, childhood, body image, or dieting) but the good news is that it is totally doable! You can learn new tastes and shed old ones. Food habits can be changed by relearning through experience. To do so, we need to become like children again: learning to eat well through example, enthusiasm, and patient exposure to good food. It is perfect timing if you have young children at home. You can start all over again with them on your side! What a great source of motivation and connection with your loved ones!

You might want to consider starting your food education from scratch with your children. You are doing it all together as a family. They are here to teach us something too. It is never too late. I know, easier said than done! But don't forget that you are a role model for your children, and they are such a good reason for making lasting changes.

*****

Invitation to Action

Take the time to ask yourself these questions:
- ✓ What are your beliefs around food?
- ✓ Is eating a burden for you?

- ✓ Do you see it as an activity that is taking some time away from doing things you love?
- ✓ Or do you see value in cooking a meal and sharing it with your family? What does "healthy" mean to you?
- ✓ Do you think there are bad and good foods?
- ✓ What is your definition of a "good meal"?
- ✓ When and how often do you eat?
- ✓ Do you multitask while you are eating?
- ✓ Do you rely on fast food restaurants and eating out to feed yourself?
- ✓ Do you use your internal cues (signs of hunger) to decide what and when you will eat?
- ✓ Is the act of feeding a dreaded prospect or do you consider it as a way to nurture you?
- ✓ Do you use food to deal with feelings like boredom, sadness, anger, procrastination, stress?

....
....
....
....
....
....
....
....
....
....
....
....
....
....

Read the book "*This Could Be Our Future - A Manifesto for a More Generous World*" by author Yancey Strickler, co-founder of Kickstarter. His book will help you widen your lens for what's important, valuable, and in your self-interest (including what food you decide to eat).

****

I Tried Making Changes But It Never Lasts

"We are what we repeatedly do."
-Will Durant, American writer, historian and philosopher

"You will never change your life until you change something that you do daily. The secret of your success is found in your daily routine."
– John C. Maxell, author, coach and speaker

If you can't make lasting changes, you are probably do something in your day-to-day that is not sustainable. You need to find a comfortable routine that is in sync with your values and intentions and that is durable in the long run. If your new habits don't fit your reality, you will end up right back where you started. Slowly and steady wins the race, right? Once you are clear with your vision and goals, start small from where you are, microstep by microstep. If you are not used to this kind of mindfulness approach around food, it might feel like a lot of work and not very natural at first. But like everything else, the more you do it, the more it becomes second nature.

When we want to make lasting changes in our life, there are four key notions to follow: Intentions (vision, big picture), Action Plan (goals), Attention, and Flexibility.

A. INTENTIONS (vision, big picture)

Let's pause for a minute and realize the power of our mind. It is our most important and efficient tool to shape the reality we want. When you **want to change your eating habits, you shouldn't start in the kitchen but rather in your head**. I would strongly recommend you start with exploring your intentions and thoughts around the food you eat and the way you are feeding your family. Look for the why behind your actions. What is the driving force behind the desire to change your eating habits?

****

Invitation to Action

Write down how you would like to feel and what you would like to see happening around your family eating habits. Don't underestimate this step as it is like a compass that will guide you in your daily decisions. If you lose the bigger picture, the rest will not fall into place.

Here are some questions and suggestions to help get you started:
- ✓ Why are you not happy about how you currently feed your family?
- ✓ What habits have been working for you? And what would you like to do differently from now on?
- ✓ What do you expect from your food?
- ✓ How do you feel about feeding your family?
- ✓ Is that a task you accomplish on autopilot mode because you are dreading it?
- ✓ Is mealtime a struggle and a source of tension for you? What could you do to make it more enjoyable?
- ✓ What do you want your family to get from the meal you prepare?

For example:

I want to provide nutritious meals for my family so they can have all the energy they need to get through their daily activities.

I want to create deeper connections during mealtime.

I want my kids to have healthy bodies, so they don't get sick often.

Once you have it written down, make it visible in your house so you don't forget about it. Also, adding a support system can be very helpful. It can be a friend, a family member, or an online support group who shares the same goals. Find a way to always remember your intentions and have some accountability.

....
....
....
....
....
....
....
....
....
....
....
....
....
....
....
....
....
....
....
....

****

B. ACTION PLAN (How you translate your intentions into day-to-day actions)
Once you have clearer intentions, it is time to create a plan for your family meals. Take into account different parameters such as cooking preferences, your family members' food preferences, restrictions, needs, and your weekly schedule between work and

after school activities (maybe some nights you won't be at home very early and a slow cooker recipe might be a good option for this kind of day)

✯✯✯✯

Invitation to Action

I invite you to take an honest look at your meal strategies. We will go more in depth with that in the Guidelines section (Part 4), but you can already start identifying some parameters:

- ✓ What do your weeks look like? Are there some regularities in terms of schedule? Include your work, your partner's work, and your kids' activities.
- ✓ What time do you come back home at the end of the day? Do you have a mid-day break when you go back home?
- ✓ How many people do you need to feed? What are their food allergies or sensitivities if they have any?
- ✓ List all the recipes you already made that you and your family feel good about.

....
....
....
....
....
....
....
....
....

✯✯✯✯

C. ATTENTION: Once your intentions and actions are clear, pay attention to your daily choices and decisions. Are the choices you are making in line with your intentions? You don't have to be perfect but be present. No harsh self-judgment here, please. We aim for progress, not perfection. Remind yourself that you are in charge of your health. You always have a choice. Being mindful will definitely help you improve your decision-making process.

****

Invitation to Action

Get away from the autopilot mode and choose mindfulness instead. It will do you so much good! Every time you see yourself hesitating, procrastinating, postponing what is important to you, the same mechanism is in play. Between the short-term benefit and the long-term benefit, your brain has decided. It will choose instant gratification. Pleasure right away. Ease right away. This mechanism doesn't say anything about you or me. It is just the way our brains work.

If you want to turn things around and make lasting changes, start asking yourself this simple yet powerful question: **What do I like best?**

- ✓ Would I rather watch one more episode now, or feel refreshed tomorrow?
- ✓ Do I prefer an extra half hour in bed, or the satisfaction of having done five sun salutations?
- ✓ Would I rather eat a bag of chips or some yogurt with fresh fruit?
- ✓ Do I prefer taking time to cook a simple homemade dinner or eating out?

Asking yourself these simple questions brings awareness to the choices you are constantly making. Because, yes, we always have a choice. And when you answer it with honesty, without judgment, or a predetermined idea of what would be the "right" or "wrong" answer, you open yourself up to your true freedom. The freedom to choose in this moment what will be best for you tomorrow, or the freedom to fully savor the pleasure available now AND not to blame yourself when the consequences reveal themselves tomorrow. Whatever your final decision is, you made this choice consciously.

....
....
....
....

....
....
....
....
....
....

****

D. FLEXIBILITY: The other important piece when you want to make some changes in your life is flexibility. Be gentle with yourself if you don't stick to your initial plan. There will always be unexpected events and you have to be ready to deal with them in a very compassionate way. If you have very well-defined intentions, setbacks will occur, but they won't destroy your long-term plan.

****

Invitation to Action

If you didn't eat the way you had planned and start beating yourself up:
- ✓ Notice your inner self-critic voice.
- ✓ Give thanks for the voice that is bringing this point to your awareness.
- ✓ Choose another thought that will bring you closer to your goal for the next meal.

Read the book *Mindful Diet: How to Transform Your Relationship with Food for Lasting Weight Loss and Vibrant Health* by Rut Wolever and Beth Reardon with Tania Hannan.

....
....
....
....
....
....
....

....
....
....
....
....

****

Making lasting changes in your life is not easy but it is possible. Our bodies are "programmed" to adapt. In France, I was trained as a neuropsychologist, and I have always been fascinated by our brain abilities. Did you know that your brain is capable of deep changes and transformation? It is called neuroplasticity. All those concerns and self-limitations are just thoughts and beliefs. As much as they seem real and true, you can always decide not to agree with them and create new thoughts that support your desire to change. You get to choose what you think. And when doing so, your brain will change its neural pathways to adjust. Mind blowing, right? And not only is your brain able to do so, but you can also count on the malleability of your taste buds. Indeed, they can be coaxed into loving the simple and less intense flavor of Mother Nature's wholesome foods, like vegetables, fruits, beans, and whole grains. When you acclimate to more wholesome food choices, your taste buds go through rehabilitation. They quickly learn to prefer those more wholesome foods, and you lose your taste for junk. Isn't that good news? So please, don't feel discouraged. It takes some time and perseverance, but it is so worth it.

In a Nutshell...

"Beliefs are the hidden scripts that run our lives. They underpin every action we take and how we interpret and respond to the world around us."
-Marie Forleo, American entrepreneur

I could have called this section "Reasons we tell ourselves to not cook." Everything starts in our head. Our beliefs are the root of our reality. The intention here is to reframe the way we think about and approach eating. If you still feel lukewarm about changing your eating habits, it is then not a good time for you to change them. Without the right mindset, you won't be able to take the necessary actions to change your eating habits. As much as you might not like your current eating situation, it is comfortable, and it is what you are familiar with. You are used to it; that's why it makes it more bearable (and hence more difficult to change). I can't force the change you are contemplating. You must hit your own version of rock bottom before you are truly ready to change. Being clear with your intentions and making sure they are in alignment with your daily life is key. Striving to simplify and remove daily decision making as much as possible will help a long way.

With this mental shift and a house always stocked with real food, you are on the right path to make lasting healthy eating habits. In the next section, I will guide you step-by-step to make those changes happen.

PART FOUR:
Guidelines to Make Home Cooking a Reality

"Healthy eating is a way of life, so it's important to establish routines that are simple, realistically, and ultimately livable."

– Horace, Latin poet

My goal here is to provide a clear, compassionate, and actionable plan to create healthy family eating habits that will serve you for life. The whole purpose of this chapter is to help you reconcile with home cooking, guiding you step-by-step to get back into your kitchen, even at the end of a long workday. In his book, *Cooked*, Michael Pollan says, "The decline of everyday home cooking doesn't only damage the health of our bodies and our land but also our families, our communities, and our sense of how our eating connects us to the world." I couldn't agree more!

I broke down this section into nine chapters. Read them in order as they build upon each other. Each of them will lead you to create better conditions to make everyday home cooking a reality, a more enjoyable experience, and ultimately a lasting habit.

I will start by helping you define what home cooking looks like for your family. Then, from re-organizing your kitchen to meal-planning, grocery shopping, cooking, eating habits, raising healthy kids, and getting successful family dinners, you will have many suggestions to get you started. At the end of each section, you have room to write down your thoughts and comments. Try to identify ideas that seem doable and fail-proof with all you have going on in your life right now. Change won't happen overnight, but instead it will build upon micro-choice after micro-choice. Once they start building up, they become very powerful and will make your life so much easier. **We are aiming for consistency here, not perfection. The key point is that those habits fit with your reality.**

Note: I want to highlight Kendra Adachi's book *The lazy Genius Kitchen*. Kendra is funny, witty, and relatable. Her common-sense advice will blow your mind in its simplicity. She is all about being a genius about things that matter and being lazy about things that don't. I love her approach and I am guessing you will too.

And, in case you need another reason or word of encouragement to spend more time in your kitchen, here is a beautiful and inspiring poem written by Joy Harjo.

Perhaps The World Ends Here

The world begins at a kitchen table. No matter what, we must eat to live.
The gifts of earth are brought and prepared, set on the table. So it has been since creation, and it will go on.
We chase chickens or dogs away from it. Babies teethe at the corners. They scrape their knees under it.
It is here that children are given instructions on what it means to be human. We make men at it, we make women.
At this table we gossip, recall enemies and the ghosts of lovers.
Our dreams drink coffee with us as they put their arms around our children. They laugh with us at our poor falling-down selves and as we put ourselves back together once again at the table.
This table has been a house in the rain, an umbrella in the sun.
Wars have begun and ended at this table. It is a place to hide in the shadow of terror. A place to celebrate the terrible victory.
We have given birth on this table, and have prepared our parents for burial here.
At this table we sing with joy, with sorrow. We pray of suffering and remorse. We give thanks.
Perhaps the world will end at the kitchen table, while we are laughing and crying, eating of the last sweet bite.

"Perhaps the World Ends Here" from *The Woman Who Fell From the Sky* by Joy Harjo. Copyright © 1994 by Joy Harjo. Used by permission of W.W. Norton & Company, Inc., www.wwnorton.com.

Define Your Home Cooking Style

Before diving into some guidelines, I want you to get clear about your current cooking situation. At this point in the book, I hope you have come to understand and agree that there is not just one way to eat healthy. You can really customize healthy eating to make it fit your lifestyle and your beliefs around food. So, I want you to take the time to check in with yourself about your cooking needs and habits. Grab a piece of paper and write down your current situation. Be very specific. Note that this is not a definitive answer. Your body is constantly changing, day to day, week to week, year to year. And it is the same for the circumstances around you. They evolve all the time. Maybe your baby is ready to start eating solid food, you are starting a new job, your kids have become busier with after school activities, your kids are leaving the nest and you have to cook for less people. Or maybe you just watched an eye-opening food documentary and you decided to make some drastic changes overnight. The picture frequently changes, and it is totally ok. Try to get an honest overview of your current life.

****

Invitation to Action

- ✓ What season of your life are you in?
- ✓ Write down your overall work schedule and your kids after school activities schedule.
- ✓ What time do you come back home? Do you work from home?
- ✓ Do you have a regular weekly schedule, or does it change every week?

- ✓ Do you keep some free time during the week or the weekend for cooking?
- ✓ When do you cook for your family?
- ✓ What days of the week is the whole family home to have dinner together?
- ✓ Make a list of the food you and your family enjoy eating, taking into account potential food allergies but also your food beliefs. Try to stick to real food.
- ✓ What is your actual cooking style?
- ✓ Are you a recipe follower or more like a freestyle-kind of person?
- ✓ Do you rely a lot on cans and packaged foods?
- ✓ What are your favorite recipes?
- ✓ How would you describe your cooking?
- ✓ Does your cooking style match your day-to-day life and your beliefs?
- ✓ If you don't have strong beliefs about what to eat and/or not eat and how to cook and eat, try to visualize your ideal home-cooking style, and write it down.

....
....
....
....
....
....
....
....
....
....
....
....
....
....

✸✸✸✸

Here is my kind of cooking style:

- Our family eats mostly a whole food plant-based diet with some animal products (poultry, meat, and fish) but in small quantities and good quality. We treat animal products like condiments and not as the main component of a meal.
- No packaged foods with a very long list of chemicals and additives. I always read the labels.
- I like made-from-scratch stuff. Items such as bread taste better homemade than store-bought versions. And once you have the right recipe, it won't feel intimidating at all, I promise (see my baguette recipe in the "Breads" section). This isn't to say that I do everything from scratch, but it is fun to learn some basics. It gives me a huge feeling of freedom and accomplishment.
- I keep things very simple, buying mostly cheap staple ingredients such as dried beans, lentils, oats, nuts, seeds and fresh produce. These are foods that don't need labels and are the closest to their natural state. I rely on spices and herbs to elevate any dish.
- I try to make healthier versions of the traditional recipes to add some extra nutrition (mac and cheese with a creamy vegetable sauce, black beans brownies...).
- Our family is ok with eating gluten. We are French after all! I bake all my bread and know exactly the ingredients I use.
- I follow the rhythm of the seasons and what my body craves: I am less hungry in the summer. I eat more stews and soups in winter and raw food when days are warmer. (Raw food is interesting. It is tasty and filled with good nutrients and a big bonus: It saves tons of time since you don't have to cook it).
- I am a lazy cook which means:
    - Easy-to-follow recipes and measurements
    - Quick recipes with a short list of ingredients

- Extra points for One-pot dishes - I am a big fan of the Instant Pot® (or any electric pressure cooker). In my opinion, one great pot dish is the basis of a great meal.
- I am not afraid of repetition. Our family doesn't mind eating the same dish regularly. We rotate among a short list of meals.
- I cook with what I have in my fridge. I have some basics in mind and don't always follow recipes. I call it impromptu cooking, and, in my opinion, it is a great skill to develop. Assembling a salad or making a stir fry with what you have in the fridge is really easy once you know the basics.
- Enjoyment during all the steps: planning, prepping, cooking, and eating. It seems odd to add it here, but it is very important to me. I don't think about cooking as a chore. It is a privilege. I am grateful to be able to serve homemade food at the table most of the time.

I hope you will make the time to assess your food situation at home. Now, let's see how you could fit new eating habits into your daily life, one step at a time. Pick whatever resonates most with you and start from there. There is no right or wrong way to do things here. I am just sharing what has been working for my family and hopefully, this will help you make the changes YOU want to implement for your specific situation.

The Art of a Functional and Practical Kitchen

A kitchen you love to use is one of the best gifts you can give yourself. It is time to be purposeful and mindful in the kitchen, from your kitchen equipment to your cookware, storage containers, plates, silverware, fridge, and pantry. Let's get an honest look at your kitchen cabinets and cupboards, shall we? How many times have you bought a new kitchen tool just because it was on sale and yet it's still in the box, untouched? Have you already bought ingredients for a new recipe you wanted to try but never got a chance to make it?

Our kitchen is often filled with things we barely use. It might not seem like a big deal at first, but I am convinced that this overloaded environment can get in our way of doing more home cooking. With basic supplies always at hand and with the right kitchen tools, you will be prepared to put a last-minute family-friendly meal together in no time. The trick now is to figure out what you can stock up on and what you can live without. We are all different in terms of how much we need to possess to satisfy our basic needs. Again, there is no right or wrong answer. It is a personal choice. Personally, I do better with a tidy kitchen, keeping just the essentials in terms of food and kitchen appliances. It is important to create a space you are willing to spend time in.

The virtues of a functional kitchen are numerous, allowing you to make home cooking a reality:
- It will save you stress as you know exactly where things are and what you have.
- It will save you time, with less last-minute trips to the grocery store.
- It will save you money, with less take-out and eating out.
- It will serve your health, with more control over what goes into your body.
- There will be less food waste. Having food staples always at hand will help you make better use of your leftovers and be more creative in your kitchen.
- A well-stocked pantry will also help you build confidence in your kitchen. The more you cook, the more you will become confident in that area. Practice makes it better (and faster), right?

Kitchen Tools, Cookware, Appliances and Dishware

My motto is "You don't need much." You don't need fancy accessories. It is better to have less but good quality. No need to accumulate kitchen appliances that you won't use on a regular basis. The "just in case" category often ends up being a "never used" category. It just adds clutter.

Basic Tools
- Set of stainless-steel pots. I have three (a small, medium and a large one).
- Dutch oven (you may think of a Dutch oven as a specialty product, but it can fulfill a wide range of cooking demands such as cooking long stews, braising, or even baking bread in the oven).
- Three pans (cast iron and stainless steel). Bonus if some of them can be transferred in your oven.
- Measuring cups and spoons. I like to have 2 sets (one for dry ingredients and one for wet ingredients).
- Cutting boards (plastic when cutting meat or fish and wooden for anything else)

- Good quality sharp knives. You just need two. A chef's knife and a paring knife. Chef's knives are great for slicing and chopping. Paring knives are perfect for smaller, more intricate jobs, like peeling, removing seeds, and slicing small fruits or vegetables.
- Vegetable peeler
- Bench Scraper (very versatile tool: scraper, trim edges of dough, knife, ruler...)
- Spiralizer (not a must, but I love using it to make zucchini noodles)
- Milk frother (not a must but great if you are into making delicious creamy drinks)
- Different-size mixing bowls
- Two thick baking sheets
- Several baking trays
- Sifter or sieve
- Vegetable steamer basket
- Rubber and wooden spatulas
- Can opener
- Oven mittens
-

Baking Tools

- Cookie cutters (I especially like a big round one to make patties)
- Two loaf pans
- Tart pans (some with a removable bottom)
- Parchment paper or silicone mats
- Silicone muffin tins
- Rolling pin

Kitchen Appliances

- Digital scale (really helpful if you love to bake)
- Food processor / high-powered blender (I have a Vitamix and in my opinion the best of the blenders)

- Electric hand mixer with an egg whisk function (when I need to separate whites from egg yolks)
- Instant Pot® or any electric pressure cooker
- Electric griddle that we use for crêpes, pancakes, tortillas
- I don't have a crockpot or a slow cooker. I didn't grow up with those. So, I don't feel the need to own one. And I usually use my Instant Pot® that has a slow cook function
- Waffle maker
- Oven

If I need a specific kitchen appliance that I don't use very often, I turn to my neighbors or close community to see if I could borrow it from them. It is actually a nice way to break the isolation and the individualist mindset some American families may be experiencing. Some apps such as MyNabes or Nextdoor can help you find or create such a community.

Dishware

We are a big family and like to host potlucks very often. Nevertheless, we don't own tons of dishware, plates, and silverware. We have enough for hosting four more people. If we have a bigger crowd coming for an informal meal, we ask them to bring their own plates and cups. It is usually well-received. With young kids around, we don't really care about owning a nice dinnerware set. To be honest, it is often a mismatch of dishes and plates from the thrift store. When our daughters were little, they used the same equipment as us. We avoid using disposable plates and cutlery trying to be mindful about our environment.

It may seem like a minor detail, but it is not: the size of our plates matters. It is known that we tend to naturally eat less when we eat from smaller plates. Consider switching from twelve-inch plates to ten-inches ones if overeating is an issue for you. Invest in a few thermos food jars for your family when you are on the go but still want to have healthy homemade food on hand. This way you can keep soups or warm dishes hot and bring them with you wherever you go. Drive through and take-out are not the only solutions when you have a packed schedule.

****

Invitation to Action

- ✓ What does your kitchen look like? How do you feel in that room?
- ✓ Do you know exactly what you have in your kitchen cabinets?
- ✓ Is it well-organized so you can easily find what you are looking for when you cook?
- ✓ Do you have enough counter space? Get rid of appliances and food items that you haven't used in months

....
....
....
....
....
....
....
....
....
....
....

****

Food Pantry Staples

Building up a well-stocked pantry is an investment that will save you time, money, and help you eat healthier. In my opinion, it is the first action to take when you are ready to change your eating habits.

Go to your kitchen, open all your cupboards, and start taking inventory. If it sounds too overwhelming or too intimidating, start with just one cupboard. Do you have many items that have been sitting on the shelves for years without ever being used? Be honest with yourself and get rid of the items you don't need for your daily cooking. If they are not expired and you feel bad about throwing them away, try to give them to a friend who will make good use of it. Among other things, we tend to overbuy spices, different types of flours, and condiments. You could start from there.

Here are the most important items I keep in my pantry, refrigerator, and freezer to make easy, healthy meals in a breeze. They're basic, versatile ingredients that are used frequently. They are usually fairly inexpensive and have a long shelf life. Your personal list may vary from mine. It will take shape over time as you begin to cook regularly and develop favorite recipes and flavors.

Cooking Oils and Fats
There are two ways to extract oils from their sources:
- Chemical process: solvents are used for this method. It usually strips nutrients and alters the composition of the fatty acids.
- Mechanical process: you extract the oils simply with pressure, in a cold setting (also called cold-pressed). The structure of the oil is not changed in that process. This second method is preferable

I like to use:
- olive oil
- coconut oil
- sesame oil
- butter
- ghee (clarified butter)
- bacon grease (I just keep the fat when I cook bacon)

How to decide which type of oil or fat to use when cooking:

High-temperature cooking	Coconut oil, bacon fat, Ghee
Low-temperature cooking	Olive oil, butter, sesame oil
Baking	Coconut oil, olive oil, butter
Seasoning	Olive oil, sesame oil

Seasoning
- homemade "Better than bouillon"
- Dijon Mustard (with no preservatives)
- rice vinegar
- apple cider vinegar
- balsamic vinegar
- soy sauce (Tamari)
- white and red wine

Spices and Dried herbs

It's easy to clutter up your spice rack by purchasing pre-bottled spice mixtures. I prefer to make my own mixes and save precious space in my pantry! You'd be surprised by how many different spice mixtures you can make from a basic, well-stocked spice pantry. In the recipe section, I offer some suggestions for different spice mixes that will make you travel.

- basil
- cayenne pepper
- chili powder
- cinnamon
- coriander
- crushed red pepper
- cumin

- curry powder
- dill
- fennel
- garlic powder
- Himalayan sea salt (fine and coarse)
- Oregano
- Paprika
- Parsley
- Peppercorn
- smoked paprika
- thyme
- turmeric

Flour and Starches

Flours with gluten

- all-purpose flour
- bread flour
- whole wheat flour

Gluten-free flours

- almond flour (you can also use almond meal, less expensive)
- arrowroot powder
- buckwheat flour (a must-have for savory gluten-free crêpes)
- cornstarch and tapioca starch
- white & brown rice flour

Baking Goods

- baking powder (super easy to make your own!)
- baking soda

- cacao powder
- chocolate chips
- vanilla extract

Sweeteners

- applesauce
- avoid all artificial sweeteners (i.e., pancake syrup).
- brown sugar
- cane sugar
- coconut sugar
- dates
- dried fruits and frozen fruits
- local raw honey
- powdered sugar (confectioner sugar)
- pure maple syrup

Grains, Beans, Lentils, and Nuts

- almonds
- black beans (I like to rotate with Navy beans, black eye peas, pinto beans)
- brown lentils
- brown rice
- cashews
- hazelnuts
- pasta
- pistachios
- quinoa
- red lentils
- rolled oats
- walnuts
- white basmati rice

Canned Goods
- black beans
- coconut milk
- diced tomatoes
- garbanzo beans (chickpeas)
- mackerel
- sardines
- tuna

Refrigerated Items
- almond milk
- apples
- bananas
- blueberry or strawberry jam
- butter
- carrots
- celery
- cheese (cheddar, mozzarella, Swiss)
- eggs
- full fat Greek yogurt or regular yogurt
- leafy greens (lettuce, spinach, kale, Swiss chard...)
- lemons
- onions

  peanut butter with no additives

  tortillas (out of the bag or toasted)

  whole milk

Frozen Items
- cauliflower rice

- chicken breasts or thighs
- corn
- fruits: blueberries, peaches, pineapple, mangos, fruit blend for smoothies
- peas
- salmon fillets
- shrimps

****

Invitation to Action

Slowly build your very own food pantry staples. Take one section at a time and create your own list. Every time you run low on one of those items, add it to your shopping list.

....
....
....
....
....
....
....
....
....
....
....
....
....
....
....
....
....

****

My top ten foods I always have at home

On any given day, I have those items in my home. They are the type of foods I lean on heavily and know how to dress, rethink, and reuse, without getting bored. We all have such a list. What is yours?

- Oats: Good for making oatmeal, gluten free flour, cookies, granola, bread, smoothies, cereal bars, savory galettes.
- Tortillas, rice wrappers, and rice cakes: if I don't have time to make bread, we use those wrappers for a quick lunch or a side for a meal.
- Avocados: perfect for layering on sandwiches and tartines, topping salads, making guacamoles, or just eating them whole with a pinch of salt.
- Nuts: walnuts, hazelnuts, cashews, pistachios. Great for granola, smoothies, energy balls, dairy-free sauces.
- Eggs: perfect for baking, soft boiled for toasts, hard-boiled for salads, scrambled for a quick meal.
- Yogurt: good for granola, smoothies, sauces, or for replacing buttermilk in baked goods.
- Fruits: delicious for snacks, salads, smoothies.
- Frozen vegetables: peas, corn, broccoli, cauliflower rice for quick stir-fries.
- Butter: I use it mostly to make clarified butter and for baking.
- All-purpose flour / Gluten-free flour blend and dry active yeast: Not super healthy but essential for bread making. Did I already say how much I love bread?
- Swiss cheese and mozzarella: two of my daughters love cheese. They could put shredded mozzarella on everything! For some reason, our family is not a big fan of parmesan.

Organization and Cleaning Hacks

Organizing Your Kitchen

No matter what size your kitchen may be, you can always maximize its function and beautify the space with a few organizational tricks.

Once your inventory is done, reorganize your pantry with the following parameters in mind:

- Don't keep food in your pantry that you are not going to use.
- Don't stock up on junk food and treats in your house in the first place so you won't be tempted when you are at home and crave sweets.
- Remember, your cabinets are not a supermarket! Don't go crazy on filling them up. Be intentional.
- Organize your kitchen cabinets so you see what you have at a glance. Avoid deep closets that are too difficult to reach in and see.
- Try to arrange items by category (beans, nuts, baking goods, spices, or oils). I like to use recycling glass jars or transparent containers to store dry goods so I can see them easily. This way I can also immediately notice when I am running low on an item. Make sure you can fit a whole bag of each item in each container, so you are not storing the jar plus a cup of leftovers in the bag.
- Use a lazy Susan to display your spices so you can easily see what you have. If you have lots of drawers, try storing herbs and spices in there using tiered racks.
- Labeled baskets and bins are a good way to store miscellaneous baking mixes and other odd ingredients.
- Think vertically. Tall cabinets are prone to wasted space up top. Don't hesitate to use dish risers, undershelf baskets for bowls and mugs, stackable containers for pantry staples, a two-tiered lazy Susan for small but frequently used items.
- Slide and seek! Slide-out shelves are also good options for your pots and pans.

- Use lid organizer racks to help you keep track.
- Add inexpensive hooks to the inside of a kitchen cabinet. Use them to store potholders and small kitchen tools. It will help you save precious drawer space.
- Add a self-adhering or magnetic towel rod.
- I use a magnetic pad on my fridge where I write my weekly menus and the basic items, I am running low on so I know what I need for my next grocery shopping. You can also use your phone to create such a list.
- I like to have a cheat sheet available anytime to help me with measurements and substitutions. Look online for "Measurement Cheat Sheets". There are tons of free resources. Here is the one I use.

Measures Equivalent	Temperatures Equivalent	Food Equivalent
<ul><li>3 tsp = 1 tbsp</li><li>4 tbsp = ¼ cup</li><li>16 tbsp = 1 cup</li><li>1 cup = 240 ml</li><li>2 cups = 1 pint</li><li>4 cups = 1 quart</li><li>4 quarts = 16 cups = 1 gallon</li></ul>	<ul><li>212F = 100C</li><li>225F = 107C</li><li>350F = 180C</li><li>375F = 190C</li><li>400F = 200C</li><li>450F = 230C</li></ul>	<ul><li>1 head cabbage = 5 cups shredded</li><li>1-pound carrots = 3 cups shredded</li><li>1 rib celery = ½ cup chopped</li><li>1 medium banana = ⅓ cup mashed</li><li>1 medium lemon = 3 tbsp juice + 2 tsp grated zest</li><li>1 medium orange = 1 about ⅓ juice + 4 tsp grated zest</li><li>1 medium onion = ½ cup chopped</li><li>3 medium potatoes = 2 cups cubed</li></ul>

****

Invitation to Action

Open your cabinets, and think about ways to better use all your space. Keep only what matters to you and get rid of the rest. Organize your pantry in a way that makes sense for you. For a thorough and customizable kitchen cabinet makeover, I highly recommend Kendra Adachi's book The Lazy Genius Kitchen, Have What You Need, Use What You Have, And Enjoy It Like Never Before.

****

Cleaning Your Kitchen

You don't need harsh chemicals or pricey cleaners to get a sparkling kitchen you enjoy using. White vinegar, baking soda and some essential oils are enough to do the job. Once you realize this, you won't need to bother with an army of household products bottles anymore. It will save you money, space and a big bonus is that it will be better for your health. Here are my favorite easy recipes for keeping the kitchen clean.

Multipurpose cleaner

Perfect to spray onto countertops, kitchen appliances, or sink using a clean cloth or damp sponge.

1 gallon recycled plastic container, funnel, tablespoon
2 tbsp baking soda
8 cups warm water
1 tbsp white vinegar
20 drops essential oils (lemon, pine, tea tree, cinnamon, eucalyptus)

Use a funnel to pour the baking soda in the container. Add warm water. In a small glass, mix vinegar with essential oils and pour it into the container. Mix well.

Homemade Dish Soap

Ditch the blue dish soap for this homemade version. Better for your health and better for the environment.

One 16 oz recycled dish soap bottle, funnel, teaspoon, and tablespoon

1 tsp baking soda
Neutral dish soap
Few drops of essential oils such as lavender, or lemon (optional)
Water

Use a funnel to pour the baking soda in the bottle. Add ⅙ of the volume of the bottle with neutral dish soap. Fill up the bottle gradually with water, shaking it regularly. Add essent.ial oils and shake again.

Notes: Baking soda is my go-to ingredient to keep my kitchen clean. I often make a paste with water to clean spills in my oven, microwave or to revive grimy baking pans. With the addition of a splash of lemon juice for acidity, my kitchen space and appliances stay spotless.

If you don't like the smell of distilled white vinegar when you are using it to clean your house, I have a pleasant hack: Keep your orange and lemon peels and add them to the white vinegar container to allow a nice scent. It works like magic.

The Art of Meal Planning: Failing to Plan is Planning to Fail

Ok, we are all different, with different lifestyles and schedules. But I am convinced that there is one thing everybody should do when one wants to provide healthy meals: planning ahead, at least a little. Planning is the cornerstone of healthy eating. I know that not everybody is on board with this but stay with me. There is a whole spectrum when we talk about planning. I am personally a very loose planner (but I will still call myself a planner)! Some food bloggers, programs, or meal plan services offer very detailed meal plans with different meals for each lunch and dinner of the week. They provide the recipes and all the grocery lists that go with it. But you don't have to go that far if you don't feel like it. It is possible to plan your meals without being too rigid. Trust me, having a frame for the week (even a very loose one) is invaluable. Preparing most of your own food is one of the single best things you can do for your health, regardless of how you choose to eat. You can control the nutrition, flavor, and quality of your food when you prepare it yourself.

Why Meal Plan?

It makes your life so much easier and less stressful. You spend less time figuring out what you are going to cook every day.
Planning allows for less food waste.

It helps you to make good choices throughout the day and the week because you thought of it ahead of time. There are less impulsive poor choices when you are hungry and need to eat.

Sticking to your plan will lead to less impulsive purchases, saving you money.

Meal planning is a wonderful tool to help you stay healthy.

What Do I Take Into Account When I am Planning My Meals?

- **My cooking style** (see previous sections)
- **What I already have at home:** I like to make a quick inventory of my pantry and my fridge and start planning my meals depending on those items first.
- **Our schedule for the week**: If your weekly evenings are loaded with kids' sports activities and late meetings, one-pot dishes using a pressure cooker or a crockpot might be a good idea. If you have a very busy week ahead it might not be a good time to plan for new recipes. More generally, ask yourself what season in your life you are currently experiencing.
- **My motivation:** It seems odd, but I often go through phases (just like with everything else). There are weeks where I clearly don't have much motivation to cook. And other times, I will try three or four new recipes in a week. Generally, I always schedule two or three lazy nights a week that don't involve too much cooking, using what I have in the freezer.
- **Seasons and the weather:** I like to be part of a CSA – community supported agriculture- or go to the farmer's market to figure out what vegetables are local and in season. When weeks are cold, my body instinctively craves warm soups. During summertime though, any type of mixed salads will do the job to feed me. I have decided to create a seasonal meal rotation. Thereby, I have about ten meals for spring and summer and 10 other meals for fall and winter.

- **Some basic food combining rules:** Food combining is the idea that certain foods pair well together, and others do not. There is a belief that combining foods improperly can lead to negative health and digestive effects. I said "belief" because it has no solid research to back it up. I am not obsessed with it, but I like to keep in mind simple rules when I create my menus for the week. I like the comparison between our metabolism and blood sugar regulation with a fire. Carbohydrates are like the twigs and sticks we use as kindling. They burn very fast. It is great to get the fire started but we can't keep them going with them without logs. The logs come in the form of proteins and fat. They burn more slowly and they are able to sustain the fire for a longer period of time without constant stockinged. In order to help fire up our metabolism to work better or burn more efficiently, it is better to eat a combination of macronutrients at every meal (carbohydrates, proteins, and fats).

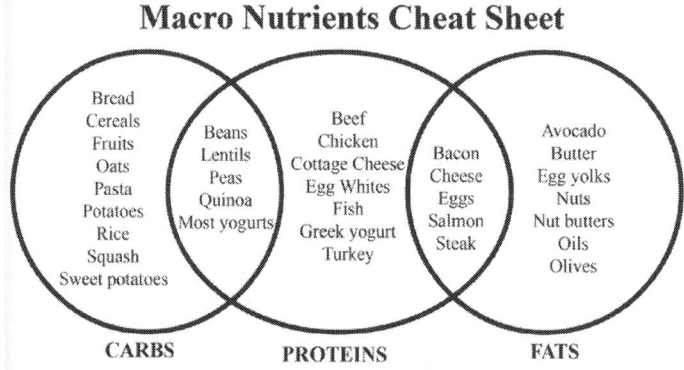

- **Our food preferences and values:** We have one daughter who has never liked animal proteins. So, most of our recipes are vegetarian and I will cook a small amount of meat or fish on the side for the rest of the family. We always use animal proteins as a condiment and not as the main component of a dish. It is a personal choice that our family has made. It supports our values around animal compassion, and it also brings down the cost of our monthly food budget.

- **And last but certainly not least, the Golden rule around meal planning is to keep meals simple!** Simplify, Simplify, Simplify! I feel like between the abundant food blogosphere, cookbooks, and TV cooking shows, we are bombarded with pictures of amazing and elaborate meals that don't really match the reality of a standard day to day family meal. One thing we could learn to do more in order to simplify our meal planning is to **learn to batch cook and embrace being more repetitive with our meals.** If you could come up with six or seven simple whole foods-based recipes per season that you enjoy and that can be made in large quantities such as soups, stews, one-pot meals, or bowls, and rotate them over the weeks, it will make your life easier. I am not afraid of being repetitive. If we have the same stew for two nights in a row it is totally OK and oftentimes it is even better the second day. Also, do not snob leftovers. Learn to reuse and appreciate them. I always feel grateful for my leftovers because they are saving me so much time. The point here is that you want dinner to be simple to prepare and simple to digest but still nourishing and fueling.

****

Invitation to Action

✓ What comes to your mind when you think about "meal planning"?
✓ Do you already have a meal plan strategy? If so, what does it look like?
✓ If you are not familiar with meal planning, how would you like to implement it?
✓ Write down a few meal ideas for cold weather and warm weather.

....
....
....
....

....
....
....
....
....
....

****

What Is My Meal Plan Strategy?

I break down my meal plan strategy in two steps:
- Once a week, before grocery shopping, I make a loose plan for our dinners, writing down three or four ideas. I am not too ambitious though and never plan to have a fresh meal from scratch at every dinner.
- Then, each morning, I do a more specific and detailed plan. Everything is happening in my head and it only takes a few minutes to collect my thoughts regarding our meals for the day. I embark on an internal dialog trying to answer a series of questions: How much time do I have? How much energy do I want to put into cooking? What do I feel like having? Who else is eating? What's the weather like? What do I have in the fridge? What can I make for lunch, snacks, and dinner?

I usually pack lunches while the girls eat their breakfast and if I have time, I do a little bit of dinner prep work before leaving the house. I like it when I can get ahead because I know I will have less work at the end of the day when I feel more tired. Sometimes, instead of doing this step in the morning, I will do it before going to bed, the night before.

The idea is to take five minutes of your time to think about the food you will consume for the day. No matter when you choose to do this during the day, the beauty of it is that once you do it, then the dreaded question "What's for dinner?" is already answered. You can forget about it for the rest of the day. It is taken care of and won't linger in the back of your mind all day. You will still have to make dinner when you come home but the mental load and decision-making process are not in the way. At the end of the day, you are just in action mode (rolling out your strategic plan), instead of last-minute-decision-panic mode (using all your energy left to decide what you will eat tonight). This easy step takes only a few minutes to do, but it will save you so much time and trouble for the rest of the day. Once you start planning, take-out is no longer your last resort when it comes to dinner time. If you do take-out, it will be because you have consciously made a choice to eat out and take a break from cooking, but not an impulsive and desperate choice.

My main meal planning work is for **dinners**. They are the most important meals for our family as we spend them all together. It is our daily social family time, and we choose to spend it around the dinner table. What makes those moments special and important is not the food we eat but the fact we are sharing the food together. It is a time for reconnection. Dinner isn't usually a feast or the heaviest meal of the day. On the contrary! We aim for an early and light dinner here, usually a one-pot dish, or a good soup with a slice of bread.

For lunch, we basically use leftovers or a combination of staples in our fridge: Buddha bowls, mixed salads, sandwiches with various spreads, tortillas or rice wraps filled with leftovers, quiche, or reheated soups. There is not much prep work for lunch. We just tap into what we have in our fridge for a quick fix but again using only real ingredients. I always make sure at the beginning of the week, I have some cooked grains, legumes, and chopped vegetables ready to go.

Breakfast is a different story. This word literally means breaking the fast from the night. Technically, you will break your fast every day, at some point. It doesn't have to be the moment you wake up, and it doesn't have to be breakfast food.

Whatever you eat first, whenever that may be: that's breakfast. Some people are hungry first thing in the morning some people are not. If you are not and your energy level is good, you may find that forcing yourself to eat when you don't want to will do more harm than good. Listen to your body's messages. I personally have been playing with different approaches over the past years, experimenting with intermittent fasting, traditional French breakfast, savory breakfast, eating first thing in the morning, or waiting to feel hungry. I tend to switch among all those options depending on my appetite and how I feel every morning. One day, I opt for fresh fruits or a smoothie. And another day, I have some bread with ghee or jam or a bowl of quinoa with kale, and scrambled eggs. My daughters opt more for a sweet breakfast: bread with butter and jam, a bowl of cereal with milk, French toast, some granola with yogurt, or porridge with fruits are some of their favorites. Some families like to rotate their selection of breakfast: smoothie on Monday, scrambled eggs on Tuesday, cereal on Wednesday… There is a lot of controversy about what's best to eat for breakfast, but I don't think there is a best way to do this. My rule of thumb is to choose good quality foods for breakfast just as you would the remainder of the day. If you leave the house without eating in the morning, just make sure you pack a health snack with you.

Snacks: My opinion around snacks has tremendously changed since my expatriation to the U.S. In France, there is this national agreement around mealtimes. We have breakfast around 7 a.m., lunch at 12 p.m., a sweet snack at 4 p.m. (called goûter) and dinner around 7:30 p.m. And in between, no snacking. Here in the U.S., snacking is the way most people eat. They don't follow a set of arbitrary mealtimes but rather eat when they are hungry. It is a big cultural difference. And it took me a long time to see any benefit to snacking. Mostly because I was witnessing people snacking on highly processed foods full of sugar, salt, and saturated fats, spoiling their appetite and leading them to skip meals. Human beings might have established breakfast, lunch, and dinner as the modern norm, a mere social convention (and not biology) but following it allows some connection time with our peers and a good regulation of our blood sugar. Snacking is ok but do it in a mindful and healthy way.

Again, it comes back to the importance of planning and being prepared. You bring an umbrella when you think it might be rainy. In the same way, we live in a climate where unhealthy food is everywhere, so just as you would bring an umbrella to stay dry on a rainy day, bring along a healthy snack so you aren't tempted to go to the vending machine and buy a bag of chips. I tend to prepare treats over the weekend like smoothies, sweet bread, muffins, and protein balls made with a variety of nuts. Then I have them available at any time during the week. Rice cakes, fresh fruits, nuts, hummus with raw vegetables, such as carrots and celery are also good options.

How Do I Proceed?

It usually takes me a couple of hours to shop and prepare some food for the week: baking muffins, cookies, making protein balls, chopping vegetables, cooking grains, beans, and legumes. Doing so, I never start a meal from scratch. I like to think in terms of FOOD prep instead of MEAL prep. It is less overwhelming. I pick a few items I already feel confident preparing and I start from there. If I have cooked grains, beans, and fresh vegetables always available in my fridge, I can easily assemble a quick healthy meal.

There are different ways to approach this: I like to do the shopping and meal-prep during the weekend. I try to make that time as enjoyable as I can. For instance, it can be a great opportunity to listen to your favorite podcast or audiobook. Sometimes, I get my husband on board to help, allowing us to connect and talk. When my kids were toddlers, I used to cook after bedtime. At that time of my life, cooking was my get away from my day-to-day life with my kids. It was quiet and I made it a meditative moment to reflect on my day and relax, doing things that I enjoy. Now, I cook more on the weekends. Depending on the season of life you are in, your strategy will be different. Like the Greek philosopher, Heraclitus said: "The only constant in life is change." Be flexible and open to experimenting. We moved to Sioux Falls, South Dakota, in 2019, and we now live very close to an Aldi store (a German family-owned discount supermarket chain). It is very convenient. And I realized it has changed our way of doing our weekly groceries. We have been doing more last-minute biking trips to the store, rather than one weekly trip. Even my older daughters enjoy running a quick errand for the family. It is an easy way to get them involved in our food consumption. I am sharing this anecdote to remind you to create strategies that are working for you and fit your schedule. Maybe some of you live in a very remote area and you do all your groceries online once a month. Start from what you are already doing and change only what is not working for you.

You can also break down the meal-prep work over the week. Some people can't or are not willing to block two to three hours of their time to spend in the kitchen. And that is totally fine! Do it your way. Use five minutes of free time here and ten minutes there. Adding them up you can accomplish quite a bit of food-prep.

For optimal nutrition and freshness, I use perishables like fresh vegetables, seafood or meat earlier in the week, and make staples like pastas, omelets, patties later in the week. Some greens like kale and chard will maintain their freshness longer than others.

Cook once, eat twice: some recipes are worth being doubled or tripled when you cook them (soups, stews, lasagnas, waffles…). Freeze a part of it or even better, do a meal swap with another family. It is such a fun and easy way to get a night off from cooking while still enjoying a delicious home-cooked meal. It is also a great opportunity to try somebody else's cooking.

Don't try new or complicated recipes every night. Some families have a weekly routine with daily themes: soup on Monday, ethnic food on Tuesday, vegetarian dish on Wednesday, breakfast for dinner on Thursday, pizza night on Friday. Maryann Jacobsen, author of *The Family Dinner Solution,* is a great resource if you want to explore this way of planning.

As you can see, there are many ways you can implement some planning into your cooking routine. Again, try to come up with a strategy that fits your life and that is sustainable. Don't be too rigid. Just try to get it done. Planning is really essential for a successful week with home-cooked meals.

****

Invitation to Action

- ✓ What meal plan strategy are you willing to try?
- ✓ Does it help to switch your mindset from Meal Planning to Food Prep?
- ✓ What ideas would you like to start implementing?

....
....
....
....
....
....
....
....
....
....
....
....
....

****

The Art of Grocery Shopping

Now that you have a few meals planned for the week, you can start writing down your grocery list and head out to the store. It is very important to have the list ready and available when you are shopping. Don't try to create your meal plan while you are pushing your shopping cart.

- **Make a grocery shopping list depending on your meal plan and the staple items you are running low on in your house**.
- **Stick to the list you created**.
- **Avoid going grocery shopping when you are hungry**.
- **Try shopping at the same grocery stores**, so you get to know them well over time. Navigation will be easier and definitely faster. Keep in mind that food retailers cleverly place key staples items, such as milk, eggs, fresh produce, along the perimeter of the store, so that you are forced to walk around the entire supermarket. How many times have you wanted to shop for just a few staples, only to leave fifty dollars poorer and feeling guilty for impulse buying? Remember, supermarkets are masters of food marketing. Everything in it (from the floor plan to the color of signage) is engineered to keep you in-store and spending more. And all too often, these tactics are not trying to make you buy fresh produce and healthy food but only the items that are not so nutritious.
- **Take the time to read the labels**. Study the ingredient list and use your own discernment. Doing so might take time and prolong your trips to the

grocery store, but the more you do it, the faster you will get. Most food manufacturers are more interested in our money than our health so do not trust health claims on packages. And actually, most of the time if there is a health claim on a package that is a sign that you should not buy it. It is important to flip products over to read the ingredient list and not make purchasing decisions solely based on the front of the package.

- **Vote with your dollars**. Choose the food you buy at the grocery store wisely. Don't let food companies dupe you. Every time you buy organic, you tell the world you want more farmers to grow healthy and safe food. Every time you buy certified fair trade, you fight poverty. Every time you don't buy packaged foods from a big food industry company, you let them know that you are not interested in their products. Every time you buy from a local farmer, think of yourself as a partner who is part of a community that values hard work, seasonality, locality, and sustainability.

****

Invitation to Action

What ideas would you like to implement when you go grocery shopping?

....
....
....
....
....
....
....

****

Now that you have a home filled with a well-stocked pantry and some delicious fresh produce, you are ready for some fun times in your kitchen.

The Art of Home Cooking

Set yourself up for success when you start cooking. Create an inviting environment: a clean and inviting kitchen, maybe a glass of wine, a fizzy drink, and some music. Music is a big thing for me. It puts me in such a good mood and disposition to spend time in the kitchen.

- If you have a buddy willing to spend time in the kitchen with you, it makes a great opportunity to catch up and share a good time together.
- When you start cooking, read the recipe all the way through the end (if it is not a recipe you know by heart).
- Have all your ingredients and cooking/baking equipment on hand before getting started.
- Clean the dishes as you go rather than at the end. Don't wait for them to pile up in your sink. While something is cooking, wash your dishes. Add some dance steps in the midst of washing and it will make the experience even better.
- Be smart in the kitchen! Every time you make more than you need, and are able to freeze or have leftovers, it is a win-win. Every time you steal a couple of moments away to boil eggs, cut fresh herbs, cut a whole pineapple, cook some grains, you give yourself a little boost for a great next meal. Congratulations! This is cooking! Next time, if you find yourself with a small block of time and don't really know what to do, use it to get ahead in the kitchen.

Block of time available:	What you can do in the kitchen:
5mn	- A quick inventory of your pantry and your fridge
10mn	- Wash and chop up fresh herbs - Wash, peel and cut carrots, celery, peppers ready for snacks or soups prep - Make dough for bread. - Peel and chop fruits for salads, or smoothies - Make an easy dip - Make salad dressings or sauces - Boil and peel eggs
1 hour (mostly cooking time, not you working for 1h)	- Cook beans - Cook whole grains - Roast vegetables

If you don't feel ready to do all the pre-steps before actually cooking (planning, shopping, and chopping), you can try a meal kit delivery service where the ingredients and recipes arrive on your doorstep (see resources p.97). Of course, this has a cost but if you can afford it, it could be a good option to get started. Just make sure to vet the company and be certain they are not offering processed food disguised as healthy food.

Practice will make this process easier and faster. As with anything, the more you cook, the better and more efficient you'll become. Even if you're a complete novice in the kitchen, you'll soon master some quick, healthy meals.

The Art of Impromptu Cooking

There is an important skill that I would like to bring up here. It is **impromptu cooking**. You do impromptu cooking when you are trying to make a meal with what you have on hand, without making an extra trip to the store. This ability requires some confidence in the kitchen along with some basic cooking skills, but once you get the hang of it, it is fun and liberating, not to mention an efficient use of your time. You even feel more pleased with yourself after putting together such a meal because you don't just follow someone else's recipe. You are going with the flow and following your intuition and creativity. Again, the more you practice this approach of cooking, the easier it will get.

Here are my basic steps for impromptu cooking:
- **I start with the vegetables** I have on hand and select a few vegetables I have in my fridge.
- Then depending on what I have available in my pantry, I decide about **the format of the meal:** Soup, roasted veggie in an oven sheet pan dish, frittata, stir fry, taco / burrito, salad.
  For instance, if the vegetables are not super fresh and I have some vegetable stock, I will make a soup and puree the whole thing for a velvety texture. If I have tortillas and beans, it will be taco or burrito night. If the veggies go well together, I will make an oven sheet pan dish with a drizzle of olive oil. A stir fry is also a good option and very easy to put together. A kitchen sink salad is a great idea if you don't feel like cooking (tossing greens with a hearty grain

and adding some roasted vegetables, with nuts and dried fruits). Or you can decide to go for a frittata (an egg-based dish you can load with vegetables).
- Then I try to look for **supporting ingredients** that will add some flavor and balance to my dish: spices, sauces, dressing, fresh herbs, a slice of avocado, sliced almonds, etc.

****

Invitation to Action

✓ Do you like cooking from scratch with whatever you have in your fridge? Or is it something that intimidates you?

✓ Do you have memories of putting a meal together with random ingredients from your fridge? How was this experience for you?

✓ Do you see the value and benefits of this approach of cooking?

....
....
....
....
....
....
....
....
....
....
....
....

****

The Art of Healthy Eating

Here are a few recommendations I have been using for my daily eating habits. They are my compass to help me make good choices when I am feeling hungry. I take in account what I eat, when I eat, and how I eat. These principles have become so integrated into my life that I don't even think about them consciously anymore. Basically, I am bringing more mindfulness around my meals.

What I eat

I don't overthink my food consumption and use my common sense. It really is that simple, but it is simply not that easy because of the culture that surrounds us. The food industry wants to keep us confused with tons of controversial nutrition facts and more new food items every day, so we keep buying and trying their products. Don't be fooled by those seductive campaigns and promises of well-being. Remember what real food is: food that grows in nature and not in labs. Eating a whole food, plant-based diet (or mostly so with animal products seen as a garnish rather than a staple) is the most realistic, beneficial, fair, and sustainable diet for most people and the planet. We should all have a predominance of plants in our diet no matter what "diet" we choose.

I eat real food and avoid packaged foods. I am committed to eating the food that my great grandparents would recognize and eat. I try to buy food that is not packaged and hence doesn't need a food label. And if I buy packaged food, I read the label carefully. The less ingredients, the better. If there is an ingredient on the list that it is not in your pantry or that you can't pronounce, don't buy it. Remember that the ingredients are listed in descending order of predominance by weight (the ingredient that weighs the most is listed first, and the ingredient that weighs the least is listed last). I highly recommend Vani Hari's website FoodBabe.com. Her mission is to investigate what is really in our food. She gives you all the information you need to read food labels correctly. Her book, *Feeding You Lies*: *How to Unravel the Food Industry's Playbook and Reclaim Your Health*, is a must-read for those who want to get some knowledge around big food companies and want to make informed decisions when shopping.

I don't eat until my stomach is full. It is the art of fueling up without filling up. Sometimes we eat as if it was our last meal. But we have to remember that we are not experiencing the food deprivation our ancestors had in the past. We live in a country of "food abundance." There is no objective fear of being deprived or feeling starved. Eat until 80% full, leaving 20% for digestion. When you overeat, you create high residue. Undigested food ferments and creates misery in the form of gas, bloating, and constipation. If you leave 20% room for digestive juices to work their magic, you will feel more balanced, and all your energy won't be used toward your digestion.

I choose water. At mealtimes, water (whether flat or sparkling) is my drink of choice (not milk or juice). Adults might opt for a glass of wine (but glasses that are not the size of fishbowls). Generally speaking, I don't drink my calories by consuming soft drinks or any type of energy drinks. I like to avoid ice cubes and stick to room temperature water. I prefer drinking water in between meals rather than when I am eating. Drinking water during mealtime dilutes stomach acids needed for digestion. It is important to stay hydrated all day long. When I feel tired, have low energy, or am feeling hungry, my first action is to drink a glass of water. Sometimes, it is just what I need to feel better! If you are not sure whether you are well hydrated or not, you can check the color of your urine. If it is pale in color, you are probably hydrated. If it is darker, you may need more fluids. If consuming plain water all day is not very appealing to you, you can flavor the water with real fruits and fresh herbs.

I try to not use food as a reward or as an emotional pacifier. When I am upset, I try not to eat, because I know that if I do, it won't do any good for me, and I will definitely make poor food choices. So, first, I try not to bring temptations home. And usually, when I have cravings, I might indulge with some of my homemade muffins, sweet bread, or protein nut balls. I am not perfect and will still succumb to my cravings from time to time, but those homemade treats are better than fueling myself with highly processed junk food. At least I know exactly what I put into my body. Overall, try to think of better rewards than food, ones that won't sabotage your body.

When I eat

I don't skip a meal and I eat at regular times every day. The only time I don't strictly apply this is when I wake up. I don't rush to have breakfast. I give my body time to wake up and ask myself what I feel like having that particular day. But for lunchtime and dinner time, I always try to aim for lunch at noon and dinner at 6:00 p.m.

I don't graze after dinner. That might be a tough one for some of you. Having dinner usually very early, you feel like it is totally normal to indulge in some snacks in front of the TV. After all, with a long day of work behind you, it is a well-deserved habit. Nevertheless, just like your mind needs a break after a long day by getting a good night's sleep, your digestive system deserves the same. I have noticed that when I want to eat something after dinner, it is usually to fight boredom or feed an emotional need that hasn't been met. It is not real hunger. So, right after dinner and cleaning up the kitchen, I have taken the habit of brushing my teeth, sending the signal to my body that I am done with food for that day.

Without knowing it, **I have been practicing time restricted eating (TRE).** Time-restricted eating means that you eat all of your meals and snacks within a particular window of time each day. Usually, the eating window in time-restricted programs ranges from 6–12 hours a day. For example, you choose to eat all your food for the day in an 8-hour period, such as from 10am to 6pm. The remaining 16 hours each day are the fasting period, during which no calories are consumed. Drinking water or unsweetened herbal teas is encouraged during that period to stay hydrated. Eating late at night disrupts the digestive clock. Doing so, you reignite your metabolism, waking the body when it is meant to slow down. If you want to know more about Time Restricted Eating, the book *The Circadian Code* by author Satchin Panda, is a great resource. He emphasizes the importance that it is not only how much we eat and what we eat but when we eat that matter, especially for long-term positive health outcomes. When you practice TRE, you align your eating schedule with your circadian rhythm.

How I eat

I eat sitting at a table. It is very important to eat at the table, and not in front of the TV, computer screen, or in your car. It is a way to acknowledge this time and make it meaningful. I would also add that I don't multitask while I am eating. I try to be intentional and focused on the food I have in front of me. If I do something else while eating, I tend to overeat.

I eat slowly and take the time to chew my food. I like to put my fork down between bites and chew my food. This one simple practice has the power to completely change your relationship with food. We pay so much attention to WHAT we eat but so many of us totally overlook the HOW, which is just as important. Food that cannot be digested (anything you swallow that isn't chewed thoroughly), is not properly eliminated, which results in bloating, weight gain, and inflammation. I often have this motto in mind as a reminder: Drink your food and chew your drink (eat slowly and chew thoroughly enough to liquefy your food and move your drink around in your mouth to thoroughly taste it before swallowing). Chewing your food correctly is the first step to good digestion. And doing so, you will also realize that you will eat less because you will feel satisfied before feeling full.

****

Invitation to Action

- ✓ Are there any points here that resonate with you?
- ✓ Do you have any other ideas to improve your eating habits?

....
....
....
....
....
....
....
....
....
....
....
....
....

****

The Art of Raising Healthy Kids

Let's see now how we can help our children eat healthier. Food education is important but, in my opinion, before even doing this, it is important to first **teach our children how to be in tune with their bodies**. Offering them the capacity to develop self-reflection and awareness around the cues their body is sending them. Letting go of some control we have over how we feed our children is a big deal and not an easy task. We haven't been taught this. For instance, have you tried to let your kids serve themselves at the dinner table? Let's be honest here, how do we know how much of a serving they really need? Why do we force them to finish their plates with the amount of food we decided to serve them? It is unfair. As long as you offer healthy food options to your kids, you can trust their judgment on how much food they need.

Be a role model for your kids. Children are natural mimics who act like their parents. Despite all the effort we put into teaching them good manners, we need to be a good example for our children. There is value in your kids watching you prepare and cook a meal. It shows that you care to provide them a healthy lifestyle. If day after day, they see you eating mostly real food, they will do the same, eventually. I am not talking about an overnight shift. It might take years before you see any "results." It is a very much a long-term approach. Maybe only years later, when your kids are adults, they will thank you for making the time to prepare meals at home during their childhood. Still, it is worth it. Don't get discouraged.

Banish convictions that kids prefer junk food and that healthy food can't be tasty. If we experience healthy food as coercion or as something requiring willpower, it will never taste delicious. It is interesting how our society tends to reward kids with junk food and sweet treats (we shouldn't call them treats by the way, as they appear regularly in most children's diets): a birthday party at school? What about cupcakes? Valentine's Day, Halloween, and Easter? The first thing that comes to mind is the amount of candy consumed on those occasions. It is total nonsense to me. Why are we sending the message to our kids that we reward them with food that eventually harms them?

Pickiness is not a personality trait; it is just a phase that kids will go through.

Kids are learning to like new foods. Our job as a parent is to make healthy food available to our children. Our kids' job is to gradually familiarize themselves with these foods. It is the concept of "Division of responsibility" created by registered dietitian nutritionist, Ellyn Satter. Her book, *Secrets of Feeding a Healthy Family: How to Eat, How to Raise Good Eaters, How to Cook*, is a great resource.

Usually when kids say, "I don't like it" they mean, "I don't know it." Eating well requires that children "tame" new vegetables. The importance of familiarity is a key food education tactic. Don't be afraid to offer the same dish over and over again, in addition with something you know they like. The more you offer it, the more likely they will give it a try and will appreciate it. Patience is your most valuable asset for this situation.

Kids are in a building phase of life. Sometimes, growing children go through phases when they need to eat more often and consume less at each meal. Be ok with it and just make sure you always have healthy options at hand. Give them choices among a wide range of healthy food. Sometimes, I like to reassure myself that my kids won't let themselves starve. If my daughters don't eat much for one meal, I am not worried. I think it is helpful to think about our food intake over longer period of time: A whole day or a whole week instead of one meal. If you have pre-teens or teen daughters, I highly recommend a book by registered dietitian nutritionist, Maryann Jacobsen, *My Body's Superpower: The Girls' Guide to Growing Up Healthy During Puberty*.

Avoid too much snacking: If kids know they can eat whenever they want, they will tend to snack more, ruining their appetite for lunch or dinner. It is ok to let them feel hungry before a meal.

Be playful: Give funny names to some dishes (witch stew, knight soup anyone?). Organize the food on the plate in an attractive way for the kids. Try to use lots of different colors. Have you already heard the saying "eat the colors of the rainbow"? All those details will contribute to making your mealtime a more relaxing and inviting experience for your child.

****

Invitation to Action

- ✓ What are your kids' current eating habits?
- ✓ What challenges around feeding your kids are you facing?
- ✓ What ideas would you like to try implementing with your children?

....
....
....
....
....
....
....
....

****

The Art of Peaceful Family Meals

Now, you have a delicious home-cooked meal ready to be consumed, and some hungry kids at the dinner table. Let's see how we can make this mealtime an enjoyable moment for everyone. Eating together creates the necessary space to pause from the hectic chaos and fast pace of the day (even if it is just for the time it takes to gobble up our plates). It is a great opportunity to look each other in the eyes and listen to one another. Often, the common experience of food encourages us to share more than the meal, but also sharing our thoughts, our victories, or challenges of the day. Eating together is valuable, no matter the age of the children. If you have an infant or a toddler, eating together offers a good food exposure. You set the tone for what is normal and expected for your family. When you have older kids, sharing a meal helps maintain the connection. I am always making sure I have at least one food on the table that the kids like. I try to aim for at least one meal a day where the whole family eats together. If dinnertime is too tricky because of after-school activities or work schedules, try breakfast. And if it is not working for your family, try once or twice a week, during weekends or whenever it is possible.

All members of the family agree on some basic mealtime rules. Every home will have its own way of doing this, and it might evolve overtime as the kids grow up. What is important is that your children know what to expect. Here is what we do in our family:

- Create a nice and relaxing atmosphere at the table: toys, books and cellphones are put away from the dining table.

- You can let your kids set the table: Napkins, plates, bowls, glasses, and cutlery. If possible, use the same tableware for you and your kids, even at an early age. You can find nice and cheap tableware in thrift stores. Use small dishes to avoid big portions.
- Use small items to decorate the table. For instance, at some point, our family uses rocks (found on a family walk). Each member has a pebble with their name written on it with a marker. We liked to use it to designate places around the table. When my daughters were younger, they loved to do that.
- Wash hands before eating.
- Create small rituals to signal the beginning of dinner: Ring a bell, light a candle, have a few mindful breaths, say a prayer, hold hands, close your eyes, or allow a few seconds of silence.
- Be mindful to not interrupt someone talking. A perfect opportunity to develop listening skills. We all have two ears and one mouth. This ratio ought to tell us something. Listening is not about hearing words; it is about hearing the message behind the words. With four kids at our table, let me tell you that it is a daily practice.
- Ask to be excused before leaving the table after the meal.
- Take the dirty dishes to the kitchen sink when you are done.
- Help with cleaning the kitchen once everyone is done.

A meal together is an invitation to reconnect and actively listen to each other. Here are a few recommendations to help you start the conversation:
- Use open-ended questions.
- Sometimes we may need some conversation starters: roses and thorns, one thing that each of us learned that day (and parents get a turn too).
- My daughters love telling jokes.
- We follow the same mindset when we have company (family visiting, potlucks…) or even if we are not home.

The Family Dinner Project website, www.thefamilydinnerproject.org, is an amazing resource to find inspiration and help make family dinners a success.

Note: When you can't be home for dinner, but still want to share a home-cooked meal, it is possible to make it happen. You can pack a homemade dinner with you: Wraps, soups, or quiches are good on-the-go options. You may want to invest in a thermos and stainless-steel container so hot foods like soups or stews stay warm. Trust me, it is a worthwhile investment.

****

Invitation to Action

- ✓ Do you have any family rituals around the dinner table?
- ✓ What would you like to see more of during dinner time?
- ✓ What ideas would you like to start implementing?

………………………………………………………………………………………………
………………………………………………………………………………………………
………………………………………………………………………………………………
………………………………………………………………………………………………
………………………………………………………………………………………………
………………………………………………………………………………………………
………………………………………………………………………………………………
………………………………………………………………………………………………
………………………………………………………………………………………………
………………………………………………………………………………………………
………………………………………………………………………………………………
………………………………………………………………………………………………
………………………………………………………………………………………………
………………………………………………………………………………………………

****

The Art of a Productive Day and the Power of Habits

Now that you have read about the steps to get more homemade meals at the table, I really want you to take action and start implementing a few ideas that seem doable for you. Make these guidelines your own and don't stop here! Make them a reality and act on it. Don't just say, "Oh, those are great ideas, but I can't implement them because [fill the blank]. The best moment to make those changes are NOW. If you wait for the perfect time, it will probably never come because there is always something going on in our lives. No matter what you think your priorities are, what you actually devote your time to is what you're choosing to make a priority in your life. Life gets busy but you have the power to choose what it is you want to be busy with. By holding yourself accountable and being responsible, you stop finding excuses and start finding solutions.

Creating new habits (and in this case, eating healthier with more home-cooked meals) starts by paying close attention to how you spend your days.

- What does a regular day look like for you?
- How do you spend your time?
- How much of your day do you spend on distractions (flipping through social media mindlessly, taking extra time to get out of bed in the morning) or maintenance (running errands, driving, getting ready, doing chores)?
- What are your current habits that are not really serving you?

Days, weeks, months can slip by so fast if you are not aware and mindful of your daily activities. The best way to be productive (rather than simply busy) is to transform some behaviors into habits. The word "habit" has a bad rep but if we consciously choose habits that are serving us well, they can have a tremendous impact and make our lives so much easier. In his book *Power of Habits*, author Charles Duhigg shares that when something becomes a habit, the brain starts working less and less. Habits free up your mental space so you can focus on what's important. Building strong habits isn't hard. It just takes some extra energy at the beginning. But once they are established, they require less effort, less energy, and less thinking to maintain. Give yourself time and grace to evolve and grow your set of habits. It is all part of the process.

****

Invitation to Action (Part 1)

- ✓ Use the Time log exercise in the previous chapter to get a better idea on how you are spending your days.
- ✓ Read *Atomic Habits* by James Clear.

****

The concept I am about to share with you is very simple yet powerful. It all starts with taking control of your day, so your day doesn't control you. In my opinion, there are two critical moments during the day that help us have better control of our lives: when one wakes up and when one goes to bed. Imagine that all the things you do during one day are beads on a string. One bead for each activity. If you tip the string, the beads easily slide off and fall onto the floor. But if you tie a knot on each end of the string, the beads stay put. Those knots are your morning and evening routines. It keeps you grounded and focused during the day, allowing you to accomplish what you had planned for that day. And it doesn't matter how unexpected and crazy things can get during the day, it's comforting to know exactly what will happen at the day's beginning and end. Not to mention that pleasurable morning and evening routines will reduce the urge to use food as your only source of pleasure. Those routines don't need to be very long to be efficient, but rather consistency and doing something that brings you joy and comfort is the key here. Five minutes in the morning and five minutes in the evening can do the trick. A morning and evening self-care ritual will look different for everyone. I'm going to give you some ideas, but only you know what will fill up your cup to create the physical and mental environments for your health to flourish.

Recipe for a good day and a healthy body

- I wake up early if I can, to have some time for myself (aka before having the kids around).

- Next to my bed, I do a few minutes of very gentle stretching. I start moving my body very slowly and gently to help it wake up (hello joints pain, as you are getting older).

- I choose a short practice such as meditation, picking one card from an oracle deck, or a quick reiki self-treatment.

- I set my intentions for the day, journaling, practicing gratitude.

- I drink a glass of water.

- I use a tongue scraper: I scrape my tongue from back to front a few times. (Did you know that your tongue mirrors your digestion, the state of your nervous system, and your organ health? Your tongue can provide you with lots of information about your health.)

- When I am in the kitchen in the morning, I quickly think about all the meals of the day and come up with a plan. I start doing some prep work if I have time.

- I drink a cup of warm lemon water, along with taking my vitamins.

- I ask my body if it is hungry. Depending on how I feel that day, I will have a different breakfast at different times of the morning. I don't drink coffee but enjoy a good cup of tea.

- During the day, I have regular hours for mealtime. I drink a lot of herbal teas or water. I always bring a mug with me wherever I go.

- I make regular breaks. If I am working on the computer, I like to regularly pause and stretch.

- I eat a light dinner: we like to have dinner around 6pm. So, we have some time after dinner to go back outside, take a walk, play games, or read.

- I brush my teeth right after dinner. So, I signal to my body that I am done with eating for the day. The kitchen is closed. Doing so I am less likely to eat before going to bed.

****
Invitation to Action (Part 2)

- ✓ Do you have a morning and/or an evening routine?
- ✓ If yes, is it working for you? What do you like the most about it? What would you like to change?
- ✓ If not, are there any practices that you are curious to try out? How could you incorporate them in your life? Be specific.

....
....
....
....
....
....
....
....
....
....
....
....
....
....
....
....
....
....
....
....

Now that you have some valuable guidelines to help you change your eating habits, let's dive into the actual cooking part. I am bringing you right into my kitchen sharing my favorite everyday recipes.

PART FIVE:
Recipes

"First we eat, then we do everything else."
-M.F.K. Fisher, American food writer

In her book, *Simple Food for the Good Life*, Helen Nearing wrote, "It has been said that there are two kinds of people in the world: those who are good cooks and those who wish they were good cooks. I hold there is a third category: Those who are not good cooks and who couldn't care less. I am happily one of those, so where do I get the nerve to write a cookbook?" I can relate to this so much. I honestly don't feel like I have an innate talent for cooking. I am not a recipe developer, nor a culinary chef. **I am just a mom who thinks cooking easy and quick everyday homemade meals for her family is important. I grew up in France where cooking and eating are an important part of the culture.**

When I was a kid, I didn't spend lots of time in the kitchen learning to cook. I just wasn't that kid interested in cooking and baking. I would rather go play outside with my friends. But I remember seeing adults around me cooking regularly. At an early age, I got the message that cooking homemade meals was the norm. Both my parents were working full time, and yet, for most dinners, they managed to put together simple homemade meals. They were not complicated and fancy meals. It wasn't a very elaborate cuisine but good enough to fuel our bodies and get the energy we needed to get through our days. They used simple ingredients (ones that didn't need labels). I didn't grow up with packaged foods and I feel immensely grateful for my parents to have raised their family this way.

I started getting more interested in putting meals together later in life, out of necessity, due to two major circumstances: becoming a mom and moving to a foreign country. Having the responsibility to feed other human beings aside from myself was very intimidating and a big responsibility that I didn't want to take lightly. As a new parent, I started questioning and second-guessing many things because I wanted the best for my children. It appears that providing healthy meals for my family became one of my top priorities. And I had to do this in a different culture than what I grew up in. When we moved to the U.S. in 2010, I had two daughters who were 5 months old and 22 months old. I wanted to reciprocate the model of cooking I grew up with, even though we were living in a different country. I still wonder if the way I cook for my family today would have been the same if we had stayed in France. Anyway, being immersed in a foreign country with young kids to feed was the time when I became a recipe hunter. I was looking for recipes that were full of flavor but most of all not time consuming and yet easy to make. In the meantime, I came to realize that I have a very loose and forgiving cooking style. It is a kind of freestyle, lazy cooking with some basic recipes in mind. Most of the time, I don't strictly follow the recipes and end up doing things my way with what I have in my pantry and my fridge. My goal is to feed modest but nourishing meals for my family, and not create a five-star menu. I love cooking but in an efficient way with the least amount of time (and dishes) possible in the kitchen. If I had the choice, I would rather read a good book on the couch or go for a walk with a friend. I just don't want to spend hours in the kitchen.

"I want to reduce food and cooking to the lowest possible denominator, to make the simplest, cheapest meals - the most easily prepared and served."
- Helen Nearing

I personally have a love/hate affair for cookbooks and food blogs. I love to learn about the authors and the stories behind the recipes. I always have a big pile of cookbooks on my nightstand to find inspiration, but I stopped buying them because I often use only a few recipes from each book. Plus, they are often a piece of art with amazing pictures that excite my palate but make me nervous to use in my kitchen, afraid I would ruin the book. And eventually, at some point, they end up on a dusty shelf. I can also be annoyed by the image of perfection those kinds of cookbooks convey. I get it! All those amazing pictures are here to make your mouth water and convince you to try a recipe. But, on the flipside, it can also make you feel like you live in a different world. Instead of feeling inspired, it leaves you feeling intimidated and overwhelmed. Another thing that bothers me is the redundancy of recipes. I don't need five different recipes for tomato sauce. My goal is to feed my family healthy meals, the easiest and fastest way possible. If I find a staple recipe that is approved by the family, it is a winner and a keeper. End of my research. I won't waste my time and energy looking for a new recipe. **I try to have ONE basic recipe for each staple dish I do from scratch and then I stick with it**. I stop looking at variations hoping to perfect it. This mindset saves me time and sanity. And when I regularly use a recipe we like, I end up knowing it by heart. And the more you do it, the more you master it, saving you time and mental energy. Practice makes it easier and faster. So, try to find ONE good recipe your whole family loves for staple foods such as pancakes, waffles, bread, quiche, soups, stir-fry, salads, and just stick with it.

I think it is very difficult to find a cookbook that exactly matches your cooking needs. Even if you find a recipe you like, you will often end up making a few changes to suit your taste. Now, I tend to borrow cookbooks from the library. If there is a recipe I really like, I write it down in a notebook dedicated to my experiments in the kitchen. And most of the time, I add personal notes on the side to make the recipes my own. Among this myriad of cookbooks, I am convinced that **the best cookbook in the world is your own**. You might need to start with someone else's recipe if you need inspiration but then make it your own. Tweak it until it suits your family's taste. In this section, you will find recipes I use the most for my family and obviously they reflect my style of cooking and my food preferences. For instance, I don't like to sauté big chunks of green vegetables and prefer to chop them very finely. For some veggies, I am like a kid, I prefer to have them mixed in a soup or a smoothie so I can't see them. Also, our family has drastically reduced our consumption of animal proteins. So, you will mostly find plant-based recipes here. Some of them might seem too simple, too plain, or too boring for you. And that is totally ok. I just want to convey the message that you can put homemade meals on the dinner table more often than you think. It is possible, and it is not that hard and time consuming.

This recipe section is definitely not like a traditional cookbook. I want to inspire you to cook things according to your taste and preferences. Don't be afraid to experiment. Just get back into your kitchen and have fun! Create a list of meals you have mastered and that your family enjoys and decide how you want to rotate them. Say goodbye to collecting cookbooks, magazines, social media, and recipe e-newsletters. Start from what you already know. Start with the recipes you already enjoy and modify them over time to fit your cooking style and family's taste.

And more than recipes, I want to give you the confidence you need in your kitchen to do more **impromptu cooking**: that is really what I want to pass along in this book. Think about when you open your fridge at the end of the week and still manage to get a decent homemade dinner at the table. Personally, when this kind of magic happens, I feel like a rock star! I love this approach of cooking because in some ways, we ignore the supposed rules of flavor combination and how we should have it right. I truly believe that cooking is an art, an art in which we can ALL participate, no matter our level of expertise or mastery.

"If you really want to make a friend, go to someone's house and eat with him... the people who give you their food give you their heart."
- Cesar Chavez, American leader and civil rights activist

Disclaimer

Writing down detailed recipes and instructions is not my forte and doesn't reflect my approach to cooking. This book is a collection of recipes I have been using for many years. Some of them are my own and others are from friends, chefs, or food blogger's creations. When I am able to, I give credit to the original developer. My intent is to show up in my kitchen every day and try things. If it is a success, it is a keeper, and if not, then I don't have to do it again. It is that simple. The recipes and instructions are not overly detailed, and I did it this way on purpose.

I want to keep things simple so you can make it your own. Proportions and exact amounts are not always given and are sometimes vague. There is a wide range within which a good dish can be made. If I could, there would have been way more of "add a little bit of that," "a handful of this," or "add this if you have it." I also didn't bother with info such as preparation time, cooking time, calories, and servings because I personally never pay attention to them. That info can fluctuate so much from one person to another: depending on your appetite, your level of comfort, and your level of experience in the kitchen. If you have a big crowd coming over, just make a bigger batch or double the recipe.

A note about using an Instant Pot® (or any electric pressure cooker)

Let the Instant Pot® be under pressure instead of you!

I have a clutter-free kitchen and a very minimalist approach regarding cooking and kitchen tools but my Instant Pot® lives on my countertop. It is by far my favorite kitchen appliance (along with my Vitamix blender). I use it every single day (no exaggeration here!). It is my grain cooker, soup/stew/broth maker, and last-minute dinner miracle marker. It is an absolute game changer. For those who are not familiar with this kitchen appliance beauty, the Instant Pot® is an electric pressure cooker but also a slow cooker, yogurt maker, rice cooker, big sauté pot, steamer, and more! What I love the most about this device is that it cooks food faster than other traditional ways to cook that specific ingredient or dish and it's all done in one pot. Plus, I can walk away while it is cooking without being afraid to burn down the house. ow does it get any better than that? The Instant Pot® meets all my criteria for simplicity. When a recipe allows for it, I will add instructions for an Instant Pot® version.

Abbreviations for the recipes

tsp = teaspoon

tbsp = tablespoon

g = grams

ml = milliliters

Self-Care "Recipes"

"One cannot think well, love well, sleep well, if one has not dined well."
-Virginia Woolf, English writer

I wanted to begin the recipe section with some of my favorite self-care practices and recipes to symbolize that you, as a mom, have to put yourself first. Taking care of yourself is so essential for the well-being of the whole family. That's where you need to start. When my daughters were still toddlers, I dealt with a severe depressive episode. I was living in auto-pilot mode, with a very low self-esteem, convinced that I had no other choice but to keep going. I believed that I should always put others first. After having three kids in three years, my hormones were totally out of whack, I couldn't really find any joy and meaning in my day-to-day life. I didn't feel in charge and in control. Life was happening without me being the conductor. I had no clue what to do in order to feel better. I felt hopeless.

Over the years, I came to realize that whether or not we implement self-care practices in our daily life depends on how much we love ourselves. Self-care all comes down to self-love and self-worth. Have you checked in with yourself recently? How much do you love yourself? How do you talk to yourself? Do you use loving, encouraging, and uplifting words? Or is your inner dialog very critical and negative? Mind and body are so connected. When learning to deeply love yourself in the first place, you come to realize that:

Your mind doesn't have to be invaded with pervasive and harmful thoughts. You get to choose what thoughts you want to make room for and pay attention to. You would never harm your body in any way. You would respect it and nurture it with nourishing food, and a healthy lifestyle.

Here are some recipes, tricks, and personal care routines that I have been implementing over these past several years to take better care of myself and support my healing journey toward a healthier mind and body.

Taking Care of Your Mind & Brain

A few years ago, I decided to think about my mind as I would think about my body. So instead of talking about mental health (that may seem very abstract), I use the expression brain health (more palpable entity). Our brain is a physical entity that needs as much attention and care as our body. Every day, we wash our body, brush our teeth, brush our hair, and give it some food and water. We have never been taught to care the same way for our mind. If our body was a car, our mind would be the engine. It is a very important piece that needs attention to be sure the car is working correctly and safely. So, you might be thinking, what does it look like when you say to take care of my brain? Well, there are different ways you could do that, but the common denominator is mindfulness. Bring awareness to what is in your mind. Simply put, pay attention to your thoughts. Stop the autopilot mode and get the control back!

Fun Exercise: A Thought Download

What you need:
your brain
one piece of paper, or a journal
a pen

Write down all your thoughts (positive and negative). Don't overthink it. Write whatever thought is on your mind. Don't try to solve them or downplay them. Let your pen flow. No room for judgment here. You are not trying to become the next Proust. Picture your paper as a dump station for your brain. By having your thoughts on paper, it is easier to have some distance and get some awareness around them. You might realize that your thoughts are not the truth and that you are simply not your thoughts.

Pay Attention to Your Inner Voice

Talk to yourself the way you would talk to your best friend. Congratulate yourself at the end of the day for what you accomplished. Be kind to yourself. I don't know anyone who found it useful to beat themselves up in order to keep going. Compassion and gentleness toward yourself are the way. Trust me.

When you start feeling some discomfort and think about reaching for the cookie jar, stop for a second. Acknowledge how you are feeling and ask yourself: "Am I really hungry?" "Will it help me feel better in the long run?" or "What do I really need right now?" And if you still end up eating those cookies, at least you will have made a conscious and deliberate decision.

Taking Care of our Body's Primary Needs: Air, Water, and Movement

Breathing (Air)

We breathe an average of 20,000 times a day, and most of the time, we don't pay attention to it, making it a primarily subconscious and automatic effort. In our culture, we have forgotten the power of conscious breathing. A few people learn how to breathe in a way that allows the body to function the way it should. Not only does proper breathing help you stay alive, but it also affects your overall health. Every system in your body relies on oxygen. Effective breathing provides you with a greater sense of mental clarity, helps you sleep better, digest food more efficiently, improve your body's immune response, and reduce stress levels. Have you paid attention to your breathing recently? I love how Amy Wright Glenn defines 'breath' in her book, *Birth, Breath and Death*, "After leaving my own mother's womb, the first thing I did was breathe in. The last thing I will do in this body is breathe out. For the living, breath is a loyal and sustaining friend. Breath takes us through spring's renewal, bright summer days, times of thanksgiving, and through the valleys of betrayal and loss. Breath knits the tapestry of time. It is the moving life force linking our entrance and exit."

Conscious breathing is a safe, easy-to-learn, and free tool to improve your health. Its power comes partly from its effects on the autonomic nervous system, which regulates the functions of our internal organs (the viscera) such as the heart, stomach, and intestines. Here are four breathing techniques you can do anytime and anywhere when you feel like a little boost of energy or need to quiet a racing mind is needed.

Note: Begin any breathing exercise with a great posture: sitting up straight allows the lungs to expand quickly and efficiently with every breath. It helps air to travel into the lungs and carbon dioxide to travel out of the lungs unimpeded. Start by taking a few natural breaths, with your eyes closed, if it doesn't bring more anxiety.

Noticing: How Do You Breathe?

How do you breathe? I got asked this odd question during my very first visit with an ayurvedic practitioner, back in Durham, N.C., in 2013. I was very surprised and not sure of how I was supposed to answer that. I learned that day that there is such a thing as reverse or backward breathing. Simply put, if you take a breath in and your stomach draws in, you're reverse breathing. And usually, this goes along with a lifted chest and/or shoulders on the inhale. When you exhale, it is the opposite: the chest/shoulders sink down and the stomach expands out. Take a few breaths and see if this rings true for you. This type of breathing is very common in our stressed and fast-paced society. But unfortunately, it doesn't support our bodies. Have you recently watched a baby breathe? When inhaling, his tummy increases in size like a balloon being blown up to a nice round shape. That's how we should do it as well. When you breathe in, expand your belly and lower your shoulders. When you breathe out, empty air from your belly, drawing your stomach in.

4-7-8 Breathing Technique

I love using the breathing technique offered by Dr. Andrew Weil:

Lips closed, breathe in silently through your nose for four seconds.
Hold your breath for seven seconds.
Make a whooshing exhale from your mouth for eight seconds.

Practice this pattern for four full breaths. It is a great breathing technique when you are struggling to fall asleep.

Kapalbhati or Skull Shining Breath

If you want to feel energized: Kapalbhati or Skull Shining Breath is a fun breathing practice that focuses on the exhale.

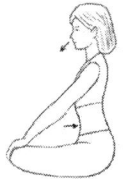

Active short, sharp/forceful exhale: Breathe out through both nostrils forcefully, so your stomach will go deep inside. (Belly in)

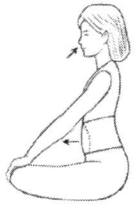

Passive, soft inhale: Breathe in deeply through both nostrils until your lungs are full of air. (Belly out)

Bhramari or Humming Bee Breath

If you want to feel relaxed and calm, try Bhramari or Humming Bee Breath.

Close your ears with your thumbs. Place the rest of your fingers on your forehead or bring them to cover your eyes. Breathe in. Breathe out with your mouth closed while you hum like a bee - Slow and audible buzz exhale.

Hydration

One of the first things I learned during my training as a Health Coach was the importance of staying hydrated. We can survive several days without eating; however, this is not the case for drinking. As the human body is made up of over 70 percent water, it depends on water to survive. Every cell, tissue, and organ need water to work properly. The color of our urine is often a good hydration indicator. If it's colorless or light yellow, you're well hydrated. If it is a dark yellow or amber color, more water intake might be necessary.

I feel like it is important to differentiate nourishing drinks with soft drinks. Growing up in France, I wasn't accustomed to drinking sodas, other than at birthday parties or when we were eating out to celebrate. Here in the U.S., sugary drinks are part of a daily beverage consumption for most Americans. It is worrisome since it is now well documented on how bad they are for our health: obesity, diabetes, addiction issues, deterioration of dental health, etc.... Try to stay away from those beverages filled with "empty calories" and if you can, replace them with healthier options. It is actually quite easy to make your own sodas using fresh fruit juice, spices, and sparkling water. I highly recommend Ashley English's book, *Quench*: *Handcrafted Beverages to Satisfy Every Taste and Occasion.*

Over these past years, I have gotten into the habit of drinking a glass of water every time I feel off. Whether I am hungry, upset, tired, or have low energy, I try to remind myself to start by drinking more water. It doesn't work all the time, but more often than not, it has proven to be effective and helpful. Water is my main drink during the day. Warm lemon water is my first morning beverage when I wake up. I started this habit more than ten years ago when it became popular, and I have never stopped since then. It provides me with a great source of vitamin C, and it helps boost my digestive and immune systems.

I don't drink coffee because I have never enjoyed the bitterness of it and since I don't do well with dairy to make it sweeter, I tend to drink tea. A simple good quality green tea will make me happy in the morning. My friends like to tease me as I always have a cup filled with tea, wherever I go. Herbal teas are a great way to get the health benefits of the plant world, too. Some of the tea bag brands I found in store were disappointingly flavorless or had a chemical taste that I didn't really appreciate. I recently discovered how easy it is to make your own blends. I am lucky to have found a "health store" in each town we have lived in since our move to the U.S. They often have a bulk section for spices, dried herbs, and teas. It is a good place to check out. And often the managers of those stores are eager to hear from their patrons about items they could add.

CCF Tea

CCF tea stands for cumin, coriander, and fennel tea. It's a traditional ayurvedic tea blend designed to soothe digestive distress and promote a very gentle detoxification. You just have to combine equal parts organic cumin, coriander, and fennel seeds, and store in a glass jar. For the best flavor, I like to roast the seeds on a baking sheet at 350 degrees Fahrenheit for about 5-8 minutes until fragrant and golden. This is optional but I find it really improves the flavor. To serve, add one rounded teaspoon per cup of boiling water. Let it steep for at least 5 minutes, then strain and enjoy. You may make big batches of this seed mix and give some to your friends.

Golden Milk

Golden milk is a traditional Indian drink that has its roots in ayurveda. In its simplest form, it is a blend of hot milk and ground turmeric. It is a delicious beverage with health benefits. This latte-like creamy drink is guaranteed to provide you the warmth you need on cold days of winter. It is ultimate self-care in a cup.

> *1 cup of cow's milk or plant-based milk such as almond milk or coconut milk*
> *1 tbsp golden paste (see separate recipe p.223)*
> *Sweetener to your taste: maple syrup, honey, or chopped dates*
> *1 tbsp ghee (optional) (See recipe page 212)*
> *Optional: dash of other spices such as cinnamon, ginger, or cardamom*

Warm a cup of milk. Add 1 tablespoon of golden paste. Stir until completely mixed. Sweeten, to taste (honey, chopped dates, maple syrup...)

Notes: I like to use a milk frother if I have one in hand to give it some extra creaminess. This is not the kind of drink you want to put in your travel mug and drink on the go, as it can stain very badly. It is definitely a beverage you want to take the time to prepare at home and slowly enjoy in your comfy clothes.

Hot Cocoa and Hot Chocolate

Hot chocolate is made with milk and melted chocolate. Hot cocoa is made with milk and cocoa powder. The latter is often considered the pauper's drink compared with the luxury of a hot chocolate.

Hot Chocolate

3.5 oz 70% chocolate

4 cups milk

Pinch of sea salt

Optional: pinch of cinnamon, pinch of cayenne, and whipped cream

Break up the chocolate bar and melt it in a pan over a water bath. Add a small amount of milk to make a thick paste. When the paste is completely smooth, add the rest of the milk and some salt. Whisk it well. Add the optional cinnamon and cayenne.

Hot Cocoa

4 cups milk

8 tbsp cocoa powder

4 tsp cane sugar (or less)

Pinch of sea salt

Optional: pinch of cinnamon, 1/8 tsp vanilla extract, and whipped cream

Put all the ingredients in a blender or food processor. Blend until it is very smooth. Pour chocolate milk into a pan. Warm it over very low heat. Ladle it into mugs and top with whipped cream (optional).

Smoothies

Surprisingly, I have never enjoyed a good smoothie until COVID-19 hit us. Those months of strict quarantine made me realize the benefits of a delicious, quick, and filling smoothie when I didn't feel like cooking a whole meal. And plus, my daughters like making them. Smoothies are a great opportunity when we want our kids to have their daily green intake. It is easy to add some leafy greens to the mix. You can get creative when you make a smoothie. One rule of thumb: the fewer ingredients, the better. No more than five ingredients is what I recommend. I usually have a combination of leafy greens, fruit, protein, fiber, and fat. This way, it becomes a nourishing nutrient-dense snack. Note: With my French roots, I haven't reached the point where I use a smoothie as a meal substitute. I am still very attached to regular meals for lunch and dinner, when chewing is involved.

Note: Juicing versus Blending - While both juices and smoothies have their benefits, I deliberately chose to only offer smoothie recipes in this book as I think they are easier to start with and faster to prepare.

Smoothie	Juice
• Need a blender. • Blend containing the entire fruits and vegetables. No waste. • Fiber creates a slow, and even blood glucose response*. • You stay fuller longer. • Easy cleaning.	• Need a juicer. • Extract water and nutrients from fruits and vegetables but discard the fiber (the pulp). • Quick absorption of the nutrients into the bloodstream. • Need to disassemble your juicer to clean it.

*Consistent blood sugar levels are paramount not only to good health, but also to daily functioning. Blood sugar dips and spikes can lead to mood swings and inconsistent energy (hello "hangry"!).

For the following smoothie recipes, add all ingredients to a blender. Blend until smooth. For the addition of liquid, feel free to choose your favorite: kefir, nut milk, oat milk, water, coconut water, juice...

Not So Moody Smoothie
1 cup frozen cherries
1 small pear
1 Medjool date, pitted

    2 tsp cacao powder

    1 tsp maca powder *

    1 tbsp almond butter

    1 cup plant-based milk such as almond or oat milk

Mango Turmeric Smoothie

    1 frozen banana

    1 cup mango, chopped

    ½ inch piece fresh ginger

    1 tbsp almond butter

    1 tsp turmeric powder

    1 tsp honey

    Water or milk for a more liquid consistency

Be Gone PMS (Pre-Menstrual Syndrome) Smoothie

(Recipe from Tnah Louise - Sacred Menarche course)

    1 banana

    1 orange

    1 cup frozen strawberries

    ¼ tsp fennel seeds

    ¼ tsp ginger powder

    ¼ tsp cinnamon

    ¼ tsp turmeric

    ⅛ tsp black pepper

    1 to 2 cups non-dairy milk, juice, or water

Apple Pie Smoothie

    1 apple

    2 Medjool dates

    1 tbsp almond butter or tahini

1 handful spinach (about 1 cup)

1 cup almond milk

½ tsp cinnamon

Berry Smoothie

1 cup frozen mixed berries

1 ½ cup almond milk

2 Medjool dates

¼ tsp vanilla extract

Green Smoothie

1 frozen banana

1 cup leafy green, spinach, kale, collard greens

1 cup chopped pineapple

1 cup kombucha, water, kefir, yogurt, or milk

1 tsp moringa** or spirulina***(optional)

*Maca is a Peruvian plant that has been cultivated for more than 2,000 years. It grows high in the Andes and has been used for its medicinal properties and more recently as a good supplement. Maca is considered as an adaptogen (a natural substance that fights stress on the mind and body and works to return systems back to "normal"). It is said to have the following qualities: boosts energy, regulates and balances hormones, gives endurance, stamina, and strength.

**Moringa has a green, earthy taste, similar to spinach, or matcha green tea. It is perfect for boosting curries, stews, casseroles, and soups. It is also a perfect addition to green smoothies.

***Spirulina is a type of blue-green algae that people can take as a dietary supplement. People consider spirulina a superfood due to its excellent nutritional content and health benefits. It gives a bright green color to your smoothie.

Exercise (Body Movement)

You notice that I use the word movement and not common synonyms such as work out or physical exercise. Whether or not you consider yourself a sporty person, body movement should be part of your daily life. **Exercise is optional, but movement is essential.** I actually consider exercise as a recent invention to counterbalance the negative impact of our modern lives. You probably already heard the saying, "Sitting is the new smoking." We sit in cars on the way to work. At work, we sit at our desks, clicking the mouse and tapping on our keyboards for much of the day. Then we come home and sit down to relax, barely keeping up with our kids' energy.

We are so disconnected from our body, that we often only notice it when something goes wrong with it. Many people consider exercising as a chore, an optional activity, or another thing to check off from their endless to-do list. There is no real pleasure for me in going to the gym, suffering while using all sorts of machines, and repeating very isolated movements. "Working out" is just an artificial way to get us to do what our bodies have known and loved for most of human history. As we evolve as a species, we are forgetting basic movements.

Movement is ancient and has always been there. Hunting and gathering, dancing around the fire, walking, climbing, running, jumping, fighting, crawling, lifting, bending, squatting, swimming, and even sex! These are all movements the human body is designed for. We don't need more exercise to remain healthy but instead, we need more movement. Once you start moving well, you also think, feel, and live well.

"To wild animals, movement is not a chore, not a temporary punishment for being physically lazy and out of shape, not an optional activity just for better looks."
-Erwan Le Corre, French American founder of MovNat,
a physical education system and lifestyle

Daily movement might look very different from one person to another, and that is fine. What matters the most is that every single day you get to move your body. There are seven basic movements the human body can do. All other exercises are merely variations of these seven: **Pull, Push, Squat, Lunge, Hinge, Rotation/Twist, and Gait/Carry**. In trying to incorporate all of these movements in your day-to-day life, you will be able to stimulate all of the major muscle groups in your body. Bonus: If you make it more playful, you'll realize that movement is not a chore, movement is life.

It can be a 5-minute stretch out of bed in the morning, walking your dog, hiking, dancing in your kitchen, a good fitness workout at your favorite gym (if that is your jam), using stairs rather than elevators, parking your car a little further away from the grocery store entrance, playing football with your children, squatting while talking to your toddler so you are at their height, wrestling with your kids, receiving a massage, and the list goes on and on.

When my daughters were toddlers, we started this daily activity we called "Fou-Fou Time" (aka crazy time). We would go on our queen size bed, or on the carpet and start wrestling together. We would get all our energy out doing it. A fun way to combine connection/touch and exercise. There were some days when the energy was more mellow and, in that case, we would snuggle and talk. We are still doing this fun family activity with my girls who are now 5, 10, 11, and 13. We don't do it every day but still pretty regularly, and oftentimes the kids remind me about doing it. Try it!

Women Body's Wisdom: Seed Cycling

Hormonal fluctuations in a woman's life are no joke and most of the time they are not addressed seriously. I am sharing about this method because I personally feel like it helped me regulate my hormonal health after I became a mom. There haven't been any published studies on seed cycling specifically. Most reports of seed cycling are anecdotal. However, there's probably little risk to ingesting seeds daily. It is worth trying as it doesn't involve super expensive supplements!

Flax, pumpkin, sesame, and sunflower seeds contain specific vitamins, nutrients, and fatty acids that are believed to support hormonal function. Seed cycling is a naturopathic remedy that involves rotating those seeds throughout your menstrual cycle. In a typical menstrual cycle, estrogen levels rise during the first half of the cycle (the follicular phase) and progesterone levels rise during the second half of the cycle (the luteal phase). Pumpkin and flax seeds are thought to support the estrogen-dominant follicular phase. Likewise, sunflower and sesame seeds supplementation are thought to support increases of progesterone in the luteal phase.

The most common method instructs women to eat 1 tablespoon each of freshly ground flax and pumpkin seeds per day for the first 13–14 days of their menstrual cycle, which is known as the follicular phase. During the second half of their cycle, which is known as the luteal phase, women are instructed to eat 1 tablespoon each of ground sunflower and sesame seeds per day until the first day of their next period when their cycle starts again. For menopausal and postmenopausal women, or women without a regular menstrual cycle, it's often recommended to use the phases of the moon as a guide to cycle dates, with day one of their cycle falling on the new moon.

Seeds used for seed cycling should be raw, not roasted or seasoned. Organic is best. For best results, try to stay consistent and eat only the seeds for the particular phase you are in (i.e., don't eat pumpkin seeds during the luteal phase).

Favorite Recipe for an Easy and Quick Cleanse: Kitchari

When I need to give my digestive system a little break, I love to make a big batch of Kitchari. Kitchari means mixture and is a delicious ayurvedic one-pot meal made with rice, beans, and spices. The softness of this savory porridge makes it easy for digestion and can work as a "cleanse" since it is also highly nutritious. I will eat this for lunch and dinner for a couple of days and will call it a "cleanse." It is a pure hug in a bowl.

½ cup basmati rice
1 cup split yellow mung beans* (or substitute with red lentils, but kitchari is typically made with mung beans)
6 cups (approx.) water or broth (see recipe p.209)
2 tsp ghee (see recipe p.212)
½ tsp coriander powder
½ tsp cumin powder
½ tsp turmeric powder
½ tsp whole cumin seeds
½ tsp mustard seeds
½ to 1 inch ginger root, chopped or grated (or ½ tsp ginger powder)
1 ½ cups assorted vegetables (optional)
Handful of fresh cilantro leaves, when serving

Put rice and mung beans in a bowl. Rinse until the water is clear. Soak the mix overnight. (Some people prefer to soak the beans for improved digestibility. However, you can skip this step without changing the recipe.) In a pot, heat ghee (or oil). Add all the spices. Pour the rice and mung beans and cover with water. Cook on medium heat until the water evaporates, about 30 minutes, stirring regularly. At the end of cooking, I like to add some chopped kale or cooked carrots.

You can keep this dish in the fridge for a couple of days. To reheat it, use a pot over the stove over a low-medium heat, adding a little water to soften and break up the mixture. Stir frequently and after about 10 minutes, it should be warmed through.
Notes: You can tailor the spice mix to suit your own needs. If you don't have whole seeds, use powders.

*Yellow mung beans are made from whole mung beans that have been hulled and split, resulting in a delicate lentil-like legume that is quick to cook and easy to digest. They're also known as moong dal or mung dal (dal means 'split').

Homemade Elderberry Syrup to Prevent and Fight Winter Viruses

The whole family loves this syrup! We call it our morning magic potion (like in Asterix and Obelix). As soon as the first signs of cooler weather appear, I give everyone a teaspoon of this syrup every morning. It is one of our favorite preventive actions to stay healthy during wintertime. I have never used fresh berries for this recipe. You can easily buy dried ones from your health food store or online.

½ cup dried elderberries (or 1 cup fresh ones)
3 cups water
1 cup raw honey
1 cinnamon stick
3 whole cloves or ¼ tsp ground cloves
1 tbsp fresh ginger or 1 tsp of ground ginger

Place berries, water, and spices in a saucepan. Bring the mix to boil. Reduce heat and simmer for 30 minutes. Use a strainer to collect the liquid. Smash the berries left on the strainer so they release the remaining juice. Let the liquid cool and stir the honey. Keep the syrup in the fridge for up to three months.
My daughters love using this syrup recipe to make elderberry gummies. You just need some gelatin powder and hot water to make them.

Elderberry Gummies

1 cup elderberry syrup - put ¼ cup aside
¼ cup gelatin powder
½ cup hot water

Mix the gelatin with ¼ cup of syrup. Add hot water to the mix. Add the rest of the syrup. Place the silicone gummy molds on a baking sheet to support them. Pour the syrup into molds (ice cube trays work very well if you don't have fancy ones). Put the baking sheet into the refrigerator and chill for about 1 hour, or until they become firm. Pop the gummies out of the molds and place into a glass airtight container with a lid. Store in the refrigerator for up to 2 months. Dosage can be from 1 to 3 gummies a day for kids 2 and over, depending on the size mold you use.

Beauty Skincare Right from Your Kitchen Cabinets

Simplicity and convenience are my mottos. I love to use ingredients I have on hand to fuel my body from the inside and outside. Your kitchen cabinet is filled with wonderful ingredients for natural skincare concoctions: coconut oil, olive oil, sesame oil, oats, cucumber, avocado, cocoa powder, honey, Greek yogurt, ground coffee beans, sugar, and more

My favorite websites for recipes and resources for natural skincare are:
- Wellnessmama.com,
- Mountainroseherbs.com,
- Banyanbotanicals.com.
- And I love the book *Homemade Beauty, by* Annie Strole.

Face

Olive Oil Eye-Makeup Remover
(Recipe from the book *Homemade Beauty* by Annie Strole)

> *2 tbsp extra-virgin olive oil*
> *1 tsp liquid castile soap*
> *¼ cup distilled water*

Combine ingredients in a small bottle. Be sure to shake thoroughly before each use. To use, apply a small amount on a cotton ball, cotton swab or pad, and gently sweep away eye makeup.

Skin Tightening Egg White Face Mask

If I am baking, I often use an egg yolk to brush bread before putting it in the oven. And I am left with an egg white. If I don't have to use it in the kitchen, I will bring it to my bathroom as a tightening face mask.

> *1 egg white*
> *Juice of ½ lemon (optional)*

Whisk ingredients together until blended and the egg whites become foamy. Apply the mixture on your face. Let sit for 10 minutes or until the mask dries. Rinse with warm water.

Avocado, Cocoa, and Honey Face Mask

This face mask is very easy to make with avocado (extremely hydrating), cocoa (excellent skin-soothing antioxidant), and honey (antibacterial and anti-inflammatory).

>   ¼ avocado
>   1 tbsp cocoa powder
>   1 tbsp honey

Mash one-quarter of an avocado in a small bowl. Stir in cocoa powder and honey and mix well. Apply the mask to your clean, dry skin for 10 minutes. Rinse with warm water.

Body

Oil Your Body

To make sure my skin keeps its moisture and stays hydrated, I like to practice a "soft version of Abhyanga," an ayurvedic practice of self-massage with warm oil. This self-care act is very nurturing. The oil is applied and rubbed into the skin to absorb in and to nourish and cleanse the tissues. It is recommended to warm the oil, but you don't have to if it feels like too much work. I like to use coconut oil during summertime and sesame oil during wintertime. It is a great opportunity for experimentation.

Scrubs

DIY scrubs are very popular and so easy to put together with ingredients you probably already have in your kitchen. Here's a soft, yet effective DIY recipe you can use to make yourself a safe face or body scrub.

>   *1 tsp brewed ground bean coffee*
>   *1 tsp granulated sugar*
>   *1 tsp olive oil*

Mix ingredients well. Rub mixture gently all over your body and/or your face. (You don't need to scrub too hard as it may cause redness and rashes.) Leave it on for a few minutes and wash off in the shower or using a washcloth.

Homemade Staples, Toppings, and Tricks That Add Some Magic to Your Cooking and Baking

There are a couple of things in my kitchen I use daily. Although they are not providing a meal in itself, they give a good kick of flavor: broth, sauces, dressings, fresh herbs, spices, and nuts can elevate any plain dish. In this section, I hope you will find some useful tips and "recipes" to make any weekday meal taste better. I also included some baking tips and shortcuts.

Spice Blends: Spice it up!

It is helpful to remember that one of the reasons packaged food tastes so good is that people who conceive it think more about the flavor than the nutrition. The food industry is becoming darn good at using artificial flavors to make their products addictive.

That being said, spices can be your best friend to add real flavor to your food. However, store-bought spice mixes can be very expensive. You can save money by making homemade spice mixes instead of buying pre-packaged ones. More and more, I notice bulk food sections in grocery stores. They are not just for rice, beans, and nuts. You can often find spices allowing you to buy as little or as much as you need. Other good places to shop for spices are ethnic food markets (Indian and Asian).

Below are a few suggestions of spice blends. You can use those seasonings on roasted vegetables, as a rub for grilled chicken, steak, tofu, in marinades, or to give a delicious and flavorful kick for your salad dressings, soups, and stews.

Whisk together all the ingredients in a small bowl. Store in an airtight container at room temperature for up to 6 months.

Moroccan Spice Blend

    2 tbsp dried parsley flakes

    2 tsp garlic powder

    2 tsp ground cumin

    2 tsp ground coriander

    2 tsp paprika

    1 tsp salt

    1 tsp ground black pepper

    ½ tsp cinnamon

    ½ tsp ground all spices

Indian Spice Blend

    2 tsp ground coriander

    2 tsp ground cumin

    2 tsp ground turmeric

    2 tsp garam masala

    2 tsp ground ginger

    2 tsp garlic powder

    1 tsp chili flakes

Mexican Spice Blend

    4 tbsp chili powder

    1 tsp red pepper flakes

    ¼ tsp cayenne pepper

    1 tsp oregano

    2 tsp smoked paprika

    2 tbsp ground cumin

    1 tsp garlic powder

    1 tsp onion powder

    1 tbsp kosher salt

    1 tbsp freshly ground black pepper

Thai Spice Blend

    2 tsp paprika

    1 tsp turmeric

    1 tsp coarsely ground black pepper

    1 tsp ground coriander

    1 tsp ground fenugreek*

    ½ tsp dry mustard

    ½ tsp ground cumin

    ½ tsp ground ginger

    ⅛ -¼ tsp cayenne powder (to taste)

*Fenugreek is less common than other spices. It tastes like a cross between celery leaves and maple syrup. You could replace it with some garam masala, yellow mustard seeds and brown sugar or just leave it out.

Fresh Herbs

The addition of chopped fresh herbs can bring so much flavor to a plain dish. My four favorites are **mint, cilantro, basil, and parsley**.

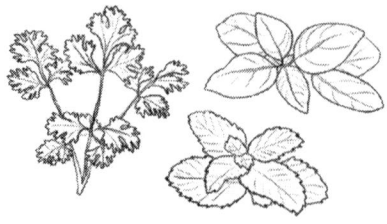

Mint can be used to make some herbal teas, or some Thai-inspired dishes, spring rolls, and homemade ice cream.

Cilantro is great for Asian-inspired meals such as curries, stir-fries, soups or Mexican-inspired meals such as burrito bowls or tacos.

Basil works well for Italian-inspired meals such as pizza, pasta dishes, or bruschetta.

Parsley has a less distinctive flavor, so I use it more for a pop of color in Tabbouleh, falafels, or salads.

You can also use a combination of those herbs to make a green sauce that you can use for anything and everything (see green sauce recipe page 210).

Tips: If you are using dry herbs, add them at the beginning of the cooking to allow for the flavor to come out. If you are using fresh herbs, add them at the end to keep the flavor.

Tips for pesto: add one or two ice cubes in your blender so herbs stay green.

Some Basic Spice & Food Pairing Suggestions
- tomato and basil (in pasta dishes, caprese salad, or bruschetta)
- poultry and thyme (this herb is a staple in French cooking)
- dill goes well with fish, potatoes, or lemons
- apple and cinnamon
- coconut milk and curry
- orange and cloves
- chiles and lime
- strawberries with balsamic vinegar

Bouillon Paste or Homemade Version of Better Than Bouillon

It never occurred to me to make my own bouillon paste until our friends Ronit and Antoine visited us from France and shared their recipe with me. She pureed fresh raw vegetables and herbs and transformed it into a concentrated paste with white wine and olive oil and preserved it with salt. I have been using this paste every week since her visit many years ago and it is so much better than any canned vegetable stock or bouillon cube I've tasted. And the best part about it? I can build on the general idea and tweak it based on what is in season and integrate my own personal preferences. It is one of those things where most people would say, "Why bother doing that myself?" But trust me. Once you have it on hand, it will give a boost of flavor to anything you want to cook. I

> *2 pounds of uncooked vegetables, washed and peeled, roughly chopped such as onions, leeks, garlic, celery sticks, celery leaves, celery roots, carrots, parsnips, shallots, zucchinis. **
>
> *Fresh aromatic herbs (parsley, thyme, herbes de Provence, tarragon…)*
>
> *Small glass of cooking white wine*
>
> *½ cup olive oil*
>
> *½ pound of salt (It is a lot of salt, but do not worry! You have to use about 20 to 25 % of the weight of the vegetables).*

*A few zucchinis are essential because they will bring some water. Don't omit them. For the other veggies though, it really depends on what you have on hand. Be as creative as you want!)
** Herbs are important in this recipe to give a good flavor. Choose your favorite. If you don't have fresh herbs, you can use dried ones.

Put all the uncooked chopped vegetables in a blender and mix well until you obtain a paste. Depending on the size of your blender, this may need to be done in batches.
Add salt, white wine, and olive oil and blend again. Transfer the mixture to a pot and cook on medium heat for about 1 hour or the time the mixture needs to reduce. Let it cool down and transfer in a jar or any container. Store in the fridge or freezer for several months.
I use 1 big spoonful per cup of liquid. I use this paste when I cook rice, pasta, quinoa, beans, and lentils. But it is also my base for making instant stock or soup. I use it

pretty much for everything to give some flavor and salt. It is so versatile! It also makes a great gift for friends and neighbors.

Homemade Vegetable Broth with Veggie Scraps

I love this "recipe." It is such a good way to use all your veggie scraps before throwing them away! Every time I peel vegetables or remove stems from greens, I keep the scraps in my freezer in a container. Once the container is full, I throw everything in my Instant Pot®, cover it with water, and boom! Done! With this frugal, flavorful, and easy homemade vegetable broth, you'll never need to pay for store-bought broth again. And if you don't feel like using vegetable scraps to make broth, you can always cover any vegetables you have on hand with water and bring it to boil.

A Few Tips for a successful homemade broth:

- Some veggies are not recommended for broth such as peppers or foods in the brassica family such as cabbage, broccoli, and bok choy.
- If you use some fresh vegetables and want to give the flavor of your broth a good kick, you can sauté some carrots, onion, celery, and garlic in olive oil or butter prior to adding the veggie scraps and the water.
- Make sure you begin with cold water and cook the broth gently at a steady simmer so the vegetables can release their flavor gradually.
- Suggestions for a more flavorful broth: dried echinacea, and astragalus root help boost the immune system. Cinnamon sticks and star aniseed provide an amazing aroma, and offer a perfect base for pho, curry, and noodle soups.
- Use about 5 to 7 prunes or dates to allow for a fuller-bodied broth.

Vegetable scraps (e.g., carrots, squash and parsnips peels, onions and garlic skin, green part of leeks and scallions, stems from kale and Swiss chard, stems from cilantro or parsley...)
Salt and freshly ground black peppercorn

1 dried bay leaf (optional)

2 tbsp salt or homemade better than bouillon

1 tbsp olive oil

Stovetop Method

Put the vegetable scraps in a big pot. Cover with water and bring it to boil. Cover with a lid and let it simmer for about 50 minutes or more. Remove the vegetable scraps using a strainer placed over a large bowl. Use the back of a spoon to press the liquid out from the veggies. Discard scraps and only keep the liquid. Additional step: Pour the remaining broth through a fine mesh strainer one last time to catch any more stray pieces.

Instant Pot® Method

Put the vegetable scraps (frozen or fresh) in your Instant Pot®. Cover with water. Close the lid and turn the valve to sealing. Press the soup button (or manual setting for 30 minutes on high pressure). When it is done, let the pressure naturally release. Open the pot and let it cool down. Collect the broth using a large bowl and a strainer to remove the vegetable scraps. Use the back of a spoon to press the liquid out from the veggies, then discard scraps. You can pour the remaining broth through the strainer one more time to catch any more stray pieces.

A good broth makes a perfect base for soups, sauces, gravy, and all kinds of recipes. And now you know how to make it from scratch in no time! Since we moved to the Midwest, I have been drinking more hot beverages during the day. I often end up filling up my thermos with this stock and enjoy drinking it on its own during the day. It might seem a little bit "whoo-whoo," but every time I drink it, I also know that I am setting good intentions and that I am nurturing my body.

Mirepoix

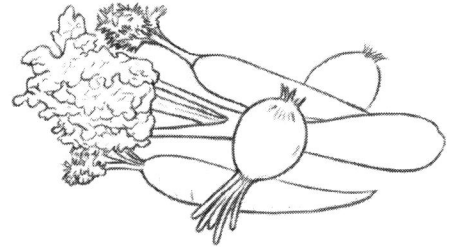

A mirepoix is an incredibly flavorful base made from humble and cheap vegetables such as onions, celery, and carrots. It is a great combination of veggies that quickly take your cooking to the next level. Any French chef will tell you that all good soups start with a mirepoix. I personally use it in many dishes. It is an excellent base for soups, stews, or a great addition when you cook rice or any other grains.

> *1 onion*
> *2 carrots*
> *2 celery stalks*
> *olive oil or butter*

Prepare your vegetables: Trim the root ends and tips from the vegetables. Rinse and scrub the carrots and celery. (If desired, peel the carrots before chopping and save root ends and peelings in a freezer-safe bag to make homemade vegetable stock later).

Chop your vegetables: The size you choose to chop them will vary depending on the recipe being prepared. However, as a general guideline:
- for sauteed recipes, chop small (¼-inch to ½-inch)
- for soups and stews, medium size (½-inch to 1-inch)
- for stock, broth, or blended soups, larger size (1-2 inches)

Cook vegetables over medium-low heat: Add the olive oil to a large skillet set over medium-low heat. Add the onions, carrots, and celery, mixing well to coat. Cook, stirring often, for 10-12 minutes, or until softened and onions are translucent. Adjust heat to prevent vegetables from browning.

My favorite way to use this mixture: Add brown lentils, broth, and a bay leaf. I throw everything (uncooked) together in the pressure cooker and in less than 20 minutes, I have a hearty stew ready to be served.

Can I freeze mirepoix? You can prepare a large batch of mirepoix ahead of time and freeze it. However, onions and celery do not freeze well. Once thawed they are mushy and somewhat unappealing. For best results, use thawed mirepoix in recipes that call for blending.

Note about onions:
- Sweet onions are best for frying. You can use them for onion rings or roasted vegetables.
- Red onions are best for eating raw. You can use them for guacamole, pickled onions, salads, chutney, or sandwiches.
- White onions are best for a good zing. You can use them for chutney, salsa, or stir-fries.
- Yellow onions are best for cooking. You can use them for soups, stews, and sauces.

Shallots are more subtle in taste and flavor. You can use them in dressings, salads, and garnishes.

Ghee or clarified butter

Ghee is one of my all-time favorite homemade kitchen items. Making your own is very simple and will save you tons of money. (Store-bought ghee can get pricey because one tablespoon of butter is lost per every five tablespoons of ghee).

Butter is composed of three ingredients: butterfat, milk solids, and water. When you remove the milk solids and water, you're left with ghee, a type of clarified butter. I like to call it "clean butter" because it is 100% pure butterfat. The absence of milk solid allows ghee to be friendly for people who are lactose and casein intolerant. It also leaves ghee with a much higher smoke point, which makes it the perfect candidate to use over high heat. Its smoke point is actually higher than most cooking oils like grapeseed, canola, and coconut oil. Ghee has a delicious browned, nutty, caramel-like taste, and aroma. It is hard to not become addicted to it. Spread a little on toast, drizzle it on steamed veggies, add it to your beverage, or simply cook with it.

1 pound / 16 ounces / 450 g of the best quality, unsalted butter you can source.

Note - You can easily double the recipe.

Gently melt the butter in a saucepan over medium-low heat, without a lid. Over the next 20-30 minutes (depending on the water content of your butter), the butter will start separating into three layers. Foam will appear on the top layer, the milk solids will migrate to the bottom of the pan and clarified butter will float between the two. The butter will make lots of sputtering sounds and perhaps splatter a bit, so be careful. Let simmer until the middle layer becomes more golden and clearer. You can remove the foam on top with a spoon so you can see the liquid.

The milk solids at the bottom will begin to brown. At this point, you can stop the simmering process, or let things progress a bit further to have more flavor. Don't wait too long though, otherwise it can burn.

When the ghee is finished, skim the top layer of foam into a bowl with a spoon and turn off the heat. Allow things to settle for a minute or so.

Pour the golden central layer through a strainer into a clean glass jar, leaving the milk solids at the bottom of the pan.

Ghee can be kept on your countertop in an airtight container for 3 months. It will become your ideal companion when traveling or going camping. You can also store it in the refrigerator for up to 1 year.

Can I use salted butter? All the resources I read say to use only unsalted butter. I tried once to use salted butter and got great results. The most important is to get the best quality of butter you can afford.

Sauces

White sauces: Roux and Béchamel

White sauces are perfect to use in a gratin, chowder, stew, pasta dish, or as a filling in savory crepes.

A roux is a mixture of equal quantities of flour and fat that's used as a thickening agent in sauces. And a béchamel is a sauce made using a roux with the addition of milk. Roux is kind of the mother sauce in French Cuisine. It is an essential building block for dishes like casseroles, chowder, or gumbo. Butter is the most commonly used fat, but you can also make roux with oil or bacon grease.

Roux

2 tbsp butter

2 tbsp flour

In a saucepan, heat the butter over medium-low until it's melted. Then, add your flour and whisk it until it's smooth (use a whisk, not a spoon). Stir it constantly to prevent burning for about 3 to 4 minutes. After cooking the roux, you'll usually add a liquid ingredient, like water, broth, or milk to make a sauce.

Béchamel

2 tbsp butter

2 tbsp flour

1 cup whole milk*

Pinch of nutmeg, salt and pepper

Warm the milk in a pan or on the microwave. Start making a roux. Add the dairy slowly, whisking in just a bit at a time until combined. Whisk constantly in a steady stream. Add nutmeg, salt and pepper. Bring the mixture to a gentle simmer and continue to whisk until the sauce thickens, about 10 minutes.

*I don't tolerate milk very well, so I often use a flavorful broth instead of whole milk to make a sauce. I use the same portion.

All-purpose Red Sauce

Some people are very serious about the difference between pizza sauce, pasta sauce, and marinara sauce. I personally don't really care and don't have time to care. For this recipe, especially during winter, I like to use diced, canned tomato. Then I add vegetables and the right seasoning to make it my own. I use this recipe mostly for making pizza, Bolognese pasta sauce, and lasagnas.

2 tbsp olive oil or ghee (see recipe p.212)

6 garlic cloves, minced

2 cups diced yellow onions (about 1 big onion)

Six 14.5 oz cans diced tomatoes

2 tbsp dried oregano

1 tbsp dried basil (you can also use ¼ cup fresh basil)

1 tsp salt (or 1 tbsp bouillon paste)

1 tbsp sugar

½ cup red or white wine (such as Cabernet, Sauvignon, Pinot Noir, Merlot), optional

2 carrots, chopped

2 celery stalks, chopped

4 mushrooms, chopped (optional)

Instant Pot® Method

Turn the Instant Pot® to sauté. Add the oil, garlic, and onions. Sauté until the onions begin to soften. Add carrots, celery, and mushrooms. Stir to combine. Stir in tomatoes, herbs, salt, and wine. Place the lid on the Instant Pot®, turn the valve to Sealing, and set the cooking time for 15 minutes on high pressure. When the cooking time is complete, let the pressure naturally release. Take the lid off and use an immersion blender to blend the sauce to your desired consistency.

Stovetop Method

Heat the oil in a medium to large saucepan. Add the onions and cook for about 2 minutes over medium high heat until translucent. Add garlic, celery and carrots. Continue cooking for about 4 minutes stirring occasionally. Pour in the wine and stir. Cook for another minute or so. Add the tomatoes, basil, oregano, salt, and pepper. Stir and bring the whole pan to a simmer. Reduce the heat to medium, cover and let it cook for about 20 more minutes, stirring occasionally. When you remove the sauce from the heat or use an immersion blender and pulse until it's smooth. Serve, can, or freeze!

All-Purpose Green Sauce

In your food repertoire, you need a white, red, AND a green sauce that will be so versatile you will be using them for anything and everything (re: dressings, marinades, dips, and spreads). From a dipping sauce to a spread for a sandwich, a condiment for fried eggs, a sauce for grilled meat or fish, or a dressing for roasted vegetables, you will be amazed by the versatility of this green sauce. I adapted this recipe from the amazing blog, Pinch of Yum.

1 avocado or ¼ cup tahini, nut butter (sunflower, almond...)
1 cup packed parsley and cilantro leaves (combined)
1 jalapeño, ribs and seeds removed
2 cloves garlic
juice of one lime (or two)
½ cup water
½ cup olive oil
1 tsp salt
½ cup pistachios (you can sub other nuts)

Pulse all ingredients, except pistachios, in a food processor. Add pistachios and pulse until desired consistency. Add water or oil if you want to thin the sauce for a dressing or a marinade. Adjust taste as needed with more lemon, salt, and pepper.

Pesto

Pesto is another green sauce/dip that is worth making. When summertime is here, we all have a neighbor, a friend, or our own garden that has basil growing like crazy. It is the perfect time to stock up on pesto for the rest of the year. I love pesto. It is such a versatile sauce. We use it in pasta, bruschetta, or rice salad. You can easily freeze it in ice cube trays and have it on hand for the rest of the year.

2 cup basil
⅓ cup walnuts
½ cup olive oil
2 garlic cloves
Salt and pepper

Blend all ingredients in a food processor.

Orange Sauce (perfect for dairy free mac and cheese or vegetable gratin)

I discovered this type of sauce on the Minimalist Baker website a few years ago. The idea is simple. You just have to mix cashews with a bunch of cooked vegetables and spices. Over the years, I tweaked the recipe to make it my own, using ingredients I often have in my fridge.

1 onion, chopped

3 garlic cloves

3 carrots, chopped (about 1 ½ cup)

2 medium potatoes or sweet potatoes, chopped (about 1 cup)

2 celery stalks, chopped

2 cups water or broth (see recipe p.209)

½ cup cashews

1 tbsp Dijon mustard

1 tsp paprika

¼ tsp cayenne pepper

2 tbsp lemon juice

2 tsp salt or homemade bouillon paste (see recipe p.207)

½ cup butter (1 stick)

Stove top version: In a bowl, pour cashews and cover it with water. Heat a pot with olive oil. Sauté onion, garlic, carrots, potatoes, and celery for about 5 minutes. Add water and salt and let it simmer for 15 minutes or until the veggies have softened. Transfer the veggies and the water from the cooking in a blender. Drain the soaked cashews Add cashews, mustard, paprika, and butter to the blender. Blend until you have a smooth sauce.

Instant Pot® version: Sauté onion and garlic with olive oil for 5 minutes. Add carrots, potatoes, celery, spices, and water. Close the lid and cook on high pressure for 10 minutes. When it is done, release the pressure manually. Transfer the cooked veggies with water in a food processor and add the rest of the ingredients: drained soaked cashews, mustard, paprika, and butter. Blend until you have a smooth sauce.

Red Lentils Coulis

If you want to add more lentils in your meal rotation but don't know how to do it, this recipe is a must-have. It's as easy and quick as cooking pasta! This is my vegetarian daughter's favorite dish. And it is a great sauce to add to any vegetables such as carrots or green beans. It's delicious whether you enjoy it warm over a bowl of rice or as a spread in a sandwich.

> *1 cup red lentils*
> *4 cups water or broth (see recipe p.209)*
> *2 tsp salt or 3 tbsp Homemade Better Than Bouillon paste (see recipe p.207)*
> *1 tsp curry powder or any other spice mixes you like (ginger, cumin, cardamom...)*

In a pan, bring the water to a boil with the lentils. You may scoop the foam forming at the top with a spoon. Reduce the heat and let it simmer until the lentils become translucent and the water is almost absorbed (about 10 minutes). Add any spices you want and mix well. Serve the coulis over rice or vegetables, adding favorite toppings: cilantro, lemon juice, crushed cashews, or peanuts.

Note: If you want to use this recipe as a sandwich spread, you may reduce the amount of water with 3 cups water for 1 cup red lentils.

Asian Stir Fry Sauce

I have two stir fry sauce recipes in my repertoire depending on what I have in my pantry. I use them when I want to make a last-minute improvised stir-fry with a bunch of vegetables. It gives it a nice Asian-inspired flavor.

Option 1

3 tbsp soy sauce

1 tbsp sesame oil

1 tsp honey

2 tsp mirin*

* Mirin is a cooking wine made from rice. You can find it in the Asian aisle of the grocery store with the soy sauce and sesame oil.

Option 2

½ cup chicken broth (or vegetable broth- see recipe p.209)

⅓ cup soy sauce

2 tbsp honey

2 tsp sesame oil

2 garlic cloves, minced

1 tbsp cornstarch

sriracha, or red pepper flakes (optional)

Combine all ingredients in a jar. Whisk or shake (with a lid on) until fully combined. Use immediately or store in the refrigerator for up to one week.

Marinades, Dressings and Pastes

It is funny because since I was a kid, I have never been into salad dressings. Oftentimes they were too vinegary for me. I have always preferred eating salads with the least amount of dressing. And then, when I started cooking more, I realized how easy it was to make your own dressing and most of all, making it the way that suits your taste buds! Don't be afraid to experiment and try this at home. Plus, you will make more room in your fridge, instead of buying countless bottles of dressings often filled with preservatives that you never finish. The homemade versions are good for your health, and good for your budget. A win-win.

Tanguy Lime Soy Ginger Marinade

I like to use this marinade on chicken, fish or tofu.

3 tbsp tamari or soy sauce
2 tbsp fresh lime or lemon juice
1 tbsp extra virgin olive oil or sesame oil
½ tsp garlic powder
½ tsp ground cumin
½ ground ginger
¼ tsp black pepper

Salad Dressings Suggestions

For each recipe below, blend all the ingredients in a blender, a jar or a bowl with a fork. Refrigerate for up to 1 week.

- Basic dressing: *1 tbsp olive oil, 1 tbsp lemon or apple cider vinegar, 1 tsp soy sauce, and 1 tbsp maple syrup (optional)*

- Balsamic vinaigrette: *½ cup olive oil, 2 tbsp balsamic vinegar, 2 garlic cloves, 2 tsp mustard, 1/2 tsp salt, and 1/2 tsp ground black pepper.*

- Asian salad dressing: *¼ cup olive oil, 2 tbsp rice vinegar, 2 tsp soy sauce, 1 tsp peeled and minced fresh ginger, 1 garlic clove and ½ tsp honey*

- Peanut butter dressing: *2 tbsp all-natural peanut butter, 2tbsp tamari or soy sauce, 2 tbsp rice vinegar, 2 tbsp maple syrup, 1 tbsp toasted sesame oil, 1 tbsp sriracha (optional for spice), 1 garlic clove, minced, and 1-inch fresh ginger, minced*

- Avocado dressing: *1/4 avocado, 1/2 lime, juiced, 1 garlic clove, a handful of cilantro, sea salt to taste, and 1/4 cup water*

Cashew Creams

Using cashews is an easy way to obtain a creamy and dairy-free all-purpose sauce. It's a perfect addition for grain bowls, soups, and salads. You can also use it as a pasta sauce, a sandwich spread, or served over roasted vegetables.

1 cup raw cashews, soaked in cool water overnight (or boil with water in a saucepan for 15 minutes)
½ to ¾ cup water*
2 garlic cloves, roughly chopped
2 tsp soy sauce or ½ tsp salt
2 tbsp lemon juice
½ tsp onion powder

Drain the cashews and rinse with fresh water. Add all the ingredients in a high-powered food processor. Blend on high speed until smooth, thick, and creamy (you might need to scrape down the sides with a silicone spatula as you go).

Flavor Variations:
- Taste and adjust for seasonings, adding more salt for saltiness, more nutritional yeast for cheesy flavor, or more lemon juice for acidity.
- Cheesy Cashew: Add 2 tbsp nutritional yeast.
- Cilantro-Lime: Replace lemon juice by lime juice and add a bunch of chopped cilantro (about 1 cup), ½ tsp smoked paprika, and ½ tsp cumin.
- Rosemary-Miso: Add 5 rosemary sprigs, 1 tbsp miso paste, and 1 tsp Dijon mustard.

*The amount of water will depend on the use of the sauce:
to drizzle onto savory foods, use ¾ cup water for 1 cup cashews

to dip or stir into soups, pasta dishes or curry, use ½ cup water for 1 cup cashews

Golden Paste

How wonderful to have a medicine chest in your own spice rack! Here is a delicious turmeric paste with tons of health benefits and different uses. Turmeric has a very long list of health-promoting benefits. It's a potent anti-inflammatory and antioxidant and may also help improve symptoms of depression and arthritis.

1–2 tsp cinnamon powder
1–2 tsp cardamom powder
1 ½ tsp ginger powder
½-1 tsp nutmeg powder
Pinch of natural mineral salt
¼ tsp black pepper
½ cup turmeric powder
1–1 ½ cups of filtered water
½ cup clarified butter (ghee-see recipe p.212) or coconut oil
Clean glass jar for storage

Mix the cinnamon, cardamom, ginger, nutmeg, salt, and pepper into a bowl and set it aside. Simmer the turmeric powder and 1 cup of water together in a saucepan on low-medium heat, stirring constantly. Once the turmeric has been thoroughly stirred in, add an additional ½ cup of water, if desired. Keep stirring until the mixture has reached a paste-like consistency. Simmer the mixture down and slowly stir in the other spices. Add the ghee and blend thoroughly. While the paste is still warm and runny, pour it into your glass container, let it cool, and refrigerate. The mixture will thicken as it cools. It may be stored in the fridge for 2–3 weeks, or frozen immediately, and thawed out at a later time if you want it to last even longer.

Great for cooking: Consider adding pinches of garam masala, salt and coriander powder to the paste to give a little boost of flavor to a dish. The amount of paste you use will depend on your personal taste and the quantity of food you are cooking. Experiment by starting low and building to your desired flavor.

Suggestions: There are many ways to use this turmeric paste. Add it to curry or stir fry. Make turmeric hummus. Use it to flavor soups or when you cook grains or beans. You can also try to spread it on a baked potato. And of course, use it for golden milk (see recipe p. 195).

Full disclosure: As good as this paste tastes, it stains very badly! Be extra careful when you use it.

Baking Tricks

Buttermilk

No need to buy buttermilk. Always have milk, lemons, and white vinegar in your pantry. One cup of milk mixed with 1 tablespoon of lemon juice or 1 tablespoon of white vinegar will do the job. We all have had the experience of sniffing a carton of milk, making a funny face, and pouring it straight to the drain. Next time you do the sniff test and are on the fence about it, use it as a buttermilk for baked goods. You won't taste the slightest bit of bitterness in the final product.

Baking powder

Mix together 2 doses of cream of tartar with 1 dose of baking soda and 1 dose of arrowroot powder.

Eggs

When you use them for baking, it is best to use the eggs at room temperature because they will incorporate into the batter better. If you forget, run them under warm water for a moment.

A good trick when you want to make a tart shell that you plan to fill with a liquid mixture is to brush the base with a lightly beaten egg white, using a pastry brush, before baking. This trick seals the crust so it stays crisp once you add the filling.

Eggs Cooking Time

- Boil the water first, then add the eggs. You have to stick close to the stove for this.
- Runny yolk: 6 to 7 minutes
- Soft jammy yolk: 7 to 8 minutes
- Creamy set yolk: 8 to 9 minutes
- Hard yolk: 10 minutes

Egg Substitute

There are different ways you can replace an egg in a recipe.

Use 1 tbsp flaxseed meal or 1 tbsp chia seeds + 3 tbsp water. Stir and let rest for 5 minutes to thicken. It should be gel-like thickness.

Use 1 tsp baking soda + 1 tbsp apple cider vinegar. Add the baking soda to the dry ingredients and the apple cider vinegar to the wet ingredients when following the original recipe. This combination is best to use in recipes that call for just 1 egg, as the more vinegar you use the more the cake will smell vinegary.

DIY Gluten-Free Flour Blend

I have never been satisfied with the store-bought gluten-free flours. So, here is an easy, 4-ingredient gluten-free flour blend to use in place of all-purpose flour in most recipes in a 1:1 ratio.

> 1 ½ cups brown rice flour
> ½ cup potato starch
> ¼ cup white rice flour
> ¼ cup tapioca flour
> 1 tsp xanthan gum (optional)

Blend together and store in a secure container in a dry place.

Different Types of Wheat Flour

Cake flour = low protein = less gluten = softest texture = great for cakes, and muffins
All-purpose flour = medium protein = moderate gluten = suitable for anything
Bread flour = high protein = more gluten formation = hardest texture = great for bread

DIY Cake Flour

Measure 1 cup of all-purpose flour. Remove 2 tablespoons. Measure 2 tablespoons cornstarch. Add to the flour. Sift together twice (sifting not only mixes the two ingredients together appropriately, but it alters the mixture, so the consistency is similar to real cake flour).

Crème Pâtissière (vanilla custard)

I have a vivid memory of my mom making this custard just for me when I was feeling down. It was my favorite comfort food. I just ate it straight out of the pot, using my finger! Nowadays, I like to use it as a filling for cakes or for fruit tarts. For an authentic flavor, I highly recommend using a fresh vanilla bean. They can be expensive and not always easy to find but if you can, choose the bean over the extract. It will be worth it!

> 2 ¼ cups milk
> 6 tbsp all-purpose flour
> ½ cup sugar
> 2 egg yolks
> 1 vanilla bean (or 1 tsp vanilla extract)
> If making a chocolate custard, add between ¼ and ½ cup grated chocolate.

Heat milk and vanilla bean or vanilla extract (and grated chocolate) in a saucepan at a low simmer. In a bowl, mix egg yolks and sugar until a pale yellow. Add the flour. Remove a small amount of warm milk and whisk with the other ingredients. Transfer back to the saucepan and cook over medium-low heat for 2-4 minutes, or until thickened. Whisk continually to prevent mixture from scalding the pan.

4-Ingredient Chocolate Spread

I was so happy when I came up with this recipe. The texture and taste are very similar to the famous brand Nutella® from Ferraro Foods. But my version contains only four ingredients and no palm oil or artificial flavoring. And most of all, there are more hazelnuts than sugar!

2 cup roasted hazelnuts

½ cup chocolate chips

1 tsp maple syrup

1 tsp vanilla extract

1 pinch salt

Blend all the ingredients in a powerful blender (Vitamix is recommended). Stop the blending process regularly and use a spatula to scrape down the edges of the container. Blend until you obtain a smooth paste.

Bread, Pie Crusts, Pizza Dough, and Crepes

BREAD

I am one of those people who can't live without a good slice of bread. Bread is a staple in France. It took me several years of expatriation before thinking I could make my own bread. Bakeries are so popular in France that most French don't bother much with making their baguettes. They just go to the closest bakery. But for French expats who live in countries that don't have good store-bought bread options, learning to make your own baguette should be a required survival skill.

I stopped buying bread in the U.S. and started making my own the day I read the ingredients for a loaf bought in a mainstream grocery store in 2016. When you know you only need flour, water, and yeast to make bread, it was such a surprise to me to see that the list was much longer. It was filled with words I couldn't even pronounce and the cherry on top is that there was paraben in it. Paraben is a common preservative more frequently found in hair and beauty products to give them a long shelf life and keep them free from bacteria. When I found out they added some in the bread I bought, it was my point of no return.

Label on the baguette I bought:

<u>Ingredients</u>: wheat flour enriched (niacin, iron, as ferrous sulfate, thiamine mononitrate, riboflavin, folic acid), water, sugar, margarine (liquid), soybean oil, partially hydrogenated soybean oil, water, salt, lecithin, mono and diglycerides, sodium benzoate (as a preservative), citric acid, artificial butter flavor, beta carotene, vitamin A, cornstarch, dough conditioners (less than 0,02%), Calcium propionate, diacetyl tartaric acid esters, contains 2% or less of L-cysteine, enzyme, ascorbic acid, corn syrup, egg wash
<u>Bakers golden finish ingredients</u>: water, soy protein, rice syrup solids, sunflower oil, propylene glycol, methylparaben and propylparaben (preservatives), acetylated

tartaric acid esters of mono and diglycerides (emulsifiers), methylcellulose, caramel color, sodium phosphate, artificial flavor for aroma enhancement, and mixed tocopherols added to protect flavor

This is quite a list, don't you think?

Making your own loaf of bread can be such a satisfying endeavor, and one that I hope every home cook can learn to enjoy. There is nothing better to me than to have a home filled with the smell of a fresh loaf of baked bread. And what a proud moment to say to yourself, "c'est moi qui l'ai fait!" (I did it myself!). Here you will find my bread recipes using dry yeast. I won't get into sourdough bread as it is a different process at the beginning.

Note about the yeast you use:
- Dry yeast comes in two forms: active and instant. Active dry yeast needs to be dissolved in lukewarm water or milk before using, while instant yeast can be mixed right into dry ingredients. You can buy yeast in individual packets or in jars, which can be great if you do a lot of baking.

    Each packet of yeast = ¼ ounce = 7 grams = 2 ¼ tsp

- Active dry yeast is the most common variety sold in grocery stores, either in individual packets or small glass jars. If using the latter, just make sure to refrigerate it after opening so the yeast stays fresh and active.

- Instant yeast is another type of dry yeast that was introduced after active dry yeast in the 1970s. it dissolves and activates faster. Sometimes instant yeast may also be marketed and sold as rapid- or quick-rise yeast. With this yeast, you can skip the first rise of the dough and shape the loaves right after kneading. Like the name implies, this type of yeast is great for quick baking projects and cuts out the added time it takes for multiple rises.

Active dry yeast and instant yeast can generally be used interchangeably, one-for-one. You just may want to consider adjusting the rise time.

Note About the Flour I Use:
The main difference between bread flour and all-purpose flour is a matter of protein. More protein in flour means more gluten can develop (and gluten is what gives baked goods structure). Bakers usually prefer bread flour for things that require more body and sturdiness, such as rolls and bread (hence the name). So, for my bread recipes, I prefer using Bread Flour (from the King Arthur Baking Company® brand) but if you don't have bread flour available, just substitute with all-purpose flour.

French Baguettes

I found out about this recipe in 2016. We had been in the U.S. for six years and I was always complaining about how hard it was to find a good bakery. I wish I had known at that time how easy it is to make your own baguette. No crazy ingredients! It's baking in its simplest form with only 4 ingredients: flour, water, yeast, and salt. You just need to invest in a baguette pan to give your baguette a professional shape.

> 2 ½ cup bread flour (or all-purpose flour)
> 1 ⅓ cup lukewarm tap water
> 2 tsp dry active yeast (or one package of active dry yeast 0.25oz)
> 1 tsp salt

Pour lukewarm water in a mixing bowl and add the yeast. Mix and let it sit for 5 minutes. Add flour and salt. Mix with a spatula until well combined. (The dough will be sticky and runny but that is fine). Cover with a wet kitchen towel and let the dough rest for about 1 ½ hours or until the dough doubles in size. (If it is a sunny day, I like to place the bowl in front of a window. It accelerates the rise time).

When the dough is ready, preheat your oven at 460° F. Place an ovenproof bowl with water on the lower part of the oven to create steam so you get a crispy result. In the bowl, mix the dough with your hands using some extra flour (you don't need much). Divide the dough into two equal pieces and shape them into logs. Lay the logs on the baguette tray, dusted with some flour. With kitchen scissors or a knife, make 3-4 cuts on the top of the logs. When the oven reaches 460° F, place the tray inside and bake for 30 minutes.

Quick Sweet Bread

Baking this bread in your oven will make your whole house smell heavenly. The honey addition gives it a brioche-kind of flavor. For this recipe, I use instant fast rising dry yeast to skip one rise. I immediately transfer the dough into the baking pan. With that shortcut, it is easy to have some fresh bread for dinner. This is by far my daughters' favorite bread.

3 cups bread flour

1 tsp salt

2 tsp dry instant yeast (or one package of instant dry yeast 0.25 oz)

1 ½ cup of warm water

¼ cup honey

2 tbsp melted butter

In a bowl, mix flour, salt and yeast. Add water, melted butter and honey to the flour mix.

Mix all the ingredients together. Place your dough in a greased loaf pan and let it rise until it fills the whole pan (about 1 hour). Preheat the oven to 400° F. Bake for 35 minutes. Wait for the bread to cool down before cutting it.

Overnight No-Knead Dutch Oven Bread

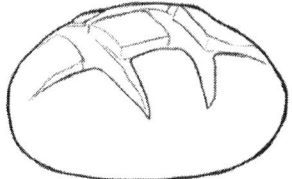

This recipe requires more time since you use less yeast. But I promise, you don't have much hands-on work (you will be asleep through most of it!). I usually prepare the dough in the afternoon or before bedtime and bake it the next day when I have some time. This is the kind of recipe that I fit into my schedule, and I love that.

3 cup bread flour
1 ½ cup warm water
½ tsp active dry yeast
1 ½ tsp salt

In a large bowl, mix flour, salt, and yeast. Add water and stir until a shaggy dough forms. Cover the bowl with a wet towel and let the dough rest for 12 to 24 hours at room temperature (it is ready for the next step when the surface is dotted with bubbles). Preheat the oven to 450° F and place a Dutch oven with the lid on into the oven. While the Dutch oven heats up, transfer the dough onto a well-floured surface. No need to knead the dough. Just fold it to form a ball. Use a knife or scissors to give a cross on top of the ball.

Place the ball on a parchment paper and place it into the Dutch oven. Cover the Dutch oven with the lid and bake for 30minutes. Remove the lid and bake for an additional 15 minutes. Remove loaf from the Dutch oven and let it cool down completely before slicing.

What To Do with Stale Bread?

Breadcrumbs

Making and toasting breadcrumbs is super easy to do at home. If your bread is still fresh, turn your oven on at 325° F. Tear the bread into small pieces above a baking sheet and toast in the oven for 15 minutes or until uniformly golden and crisp. When ready, let it cool down, and transfer the pieces of bread in a food processor and pulse until they are ground.

Whenever I have bread that begins to go stale, I rip it up into pieces and put it in a bag in the freezer. Any type of bread goes into that bag: pita bread, rolls, buns, bagels, white bread, baguette, and whole wheat bread. When the bag is full, I make breadcrumbs simply using a blender.

Croutons

Cut bread into cubes using a small cutter. Place the cubes on a broiler rack, brush with a little olive oil, and broil until golden on both sides. You can also fry the cubes on a stove, in a pan.

French Toast (see recipe p.249)

PIE CRUSTS AND PIZZA CRUST

Every great pie begins with a great crust. I think everyone needs from-scratch pie crust recipes in their arsenal. What if you want a pie right now and can't get to the store?

Trust me, it is not that intimidating or difficult. In this section, you'll find my favorite sweet and savory pie crusts recipes. Here are a few tips for a successful pie crust:

Par-baking consists of partially baking a bottom crust before filling it.
Blind-baking consists of fully baking a bottom crust before filling it.
Use cool ingredients (butter, water) and work your dough with cool hands.
Chill the dough after mixing. One of the most important things for making a great pie crust is to keep it cool before it goes in the oven. After rolling the dough out, return it to the refrigerator (or 30 minutes in the freezer) while you are making your filling.
Wait for the oven to be fully preheated before baking the pie. Remember this saying: Make it cold, bake it hot, and you will be just fine.
Use pie weights when you blind-bake your dough. If you don't, the dough will shrink considerably, and will puff up. In my baking cabinet, I always have a jar of cheap dried beans that I only use as weights to bake pie crusts. I usually fill the empty crust with parchment paper and beans. Be sure to let the beans cool down before returning them to the jar.
To keep the crust from puffing up as it bakes, pierce the bottom and sides with a fork.
To prevent a soggy bottom crust when you use particularly watery fillings, cover the crust with a lightly beaten egg white, using a pastry brush, and blind or par-bake the crust.

Basic Savory Pie Crust (Pâte Brisée)

My favorite pie crust recipe is straightforward. You can make it ahead of time and it also freezes very well. This is the one I make most of the time as I can use it for savory or sweet pies. I use my hands to make this dough, but you are welcome to use your blender if you prefer.

Makes dough for one double-crust pie, or two 9-inch pies
    2 ½ cups all-purpose flour
    1 stick butter (½ cup), chilled and cubed

⅔ cup cold water

1 egg

½ tsp salt

Mix flour and salt together in a medium-large bowl. Incorporate the butter (you should still have some rather large bits of butter when you are done). Add the egg. Slowly drizzle with cold water. Use a spoon or your hands and stir until the dough begins to clump. Transfer the dough onto a floured surface, and using your hands, fold it into itself. The dough should come together easily and not be too sticky. Divide the dough in half, shape it into two balls. Refrigerate for at least 30 minutes.

Olive Oil Tart Dough

This is a great recipe dough for people who want to avoid dairy products. If I don't have butter, I use that recipe in place of the basic savory pie crust.

Makes two 9-inch pies or one 12-inch pie

2 ½ cups all-purpose flour

⅓ cup best possible olive oil

½ cup cold water

1 tsp salt

Mix all the ingredients together in a bowl. (If the dough doesn't stay together, add a little bit of iced water). Divide the dough in half if planning to make two tarts. Roll each half in a ball and flatten it into a disk. Lightly grease a 9-inch pie dish and lay the crust in it. Trim the excess with a sharp knife. Prick the bottom a few times with a fork. Let it chill in the refrigerator for 30 minutes. If you don't use all the dough, store it in the freezer.

Sweet Pie Crust (Shortbread Crust or Pâte Sablée)

I love this recipe for apple pie or any fruit pies. You can use your hands or choose to make the dough in your blender but be careful to not overwork the dough.

1 ½ cup all-purpose flour
¼ cup sugar
½ cup or 1 stick butter (cut into small pieces)
1 egg
½ tsp vanilla extract or almond extract (optional)
⅛ tsp salt

In a large bowl, stir together flour, sugar, and salt. Add the butter to the flour mixture. Use your hands to mix until the texture resembles coarse cornmeal. Add the egg, extract, and mix until the dough pulls together. Mix to combine all the ingredients and as soon as you see that the dough forms stop mixing otherwise it will become too elastic. Cool 30 minutes in the refrigerator for the butter to firm up.

No Bake Pie Crust

I discovered this type of pie crust while living in the U.S. I never thought of using graham crackers or cookies to make a pie crust. But it is such an easy way to have some flavorful crust for pies that don't need to be baked. It is the perfect recipe for just about any cream or custard filling you can imagine.

Makes one 9-inch-deep dish plate

10 ounces gingersnap cookies (about 2 ½ cups)
½ tsp salt
½ cup or 1 stick butter,
½ tsp salt
½ cup or 1 stick butter, soft or melted

Crush the gingersnaps by pulsing them in a food processor. Or you can also place them in a plastic freezer bag and roll over them with a rolling pin. Combine the crushed gingersnaps with the butter in a medium-size bowl. Press the mixture into the pan. Cover the bottom fully and press the crumbs halfway up the sides. Refrigerate or put in the freezer for at least 30 minutes.

Notes: If you use graham crackers, follow the same recipe, and add one tablespoon of granulated sugar.

15-minute Pizza Dough

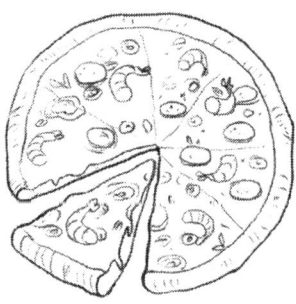

Our family loves pizza. Every Saturday night is pizza/movie night at our house. And homemade pizza is on the menu. It is so easy to make your own. This recipe calls for instant dry yeast to accelerate the rising process so you can start baking your pizza as soon as you have gathered all the toppings you need.

Makes 2 pizza crusts
- *2 cups bread flour*
- *1 tsp salt*
- *1 tbsp instant dry yeast*
- *3 tbsp olive oil*
- *1 cup hot tap water*

Preheat your oven to 500° F. If you use a food processor, place all the ingredients in the bowl and blend in "dough mode" (or use a dough hook) until it holds into a ball. Use some extra flour so the dough is not too sticky and shape it in a ball. If you use only your hands, add the flour gradually, until you obtain a smooth dough. Let it rest in a bowl while you are prepping your toppings. Divide the dough into 2 balls. Use a rolling pin to stretch the dough and form 2 discs. Place each disc on a piece of parchment paper and place them on a baking sheet or pizza dish. Add tomato sauce, pesto, or white sauce and cover with the toppings of your choice. Bake in the oven for about 20 minutes.

CREPES, DOSAS, AND FLATBREAD

Every culture has its crepe, pancake, tortilla, or flatbread. Here are some recipes for naan, dosas and crêpes.

4-Ingredient Naan bread

Adding tangy yogurt to the dough is an easy way to boost flavor. It also makes the dough more tender and easier to work with.

> *1 ¾ cup all-purpose flour*
>
> *1 ½ tsp salt*
>
> *1 tbsp baking powder (see recipe p.225)*
>
> *1 cup Greek yogurt*

In a large mixing bowl, combine 1 ¾ cup flour, salt, and baking powder. Add Greek yogurt. Mix well, until combined. Then, use your hands to form a large ball of dough. Lightly flour a kitchen surface. Flatten the dough into a circular shape and divide into 8 even portions. Flatten each portion into a rectangular shape. Cook them in a saucepan on medium heat.

Once cooked, if desired, brush the tops of each naan bread with melted butter or ghee.

Dosas

Dosa is a popular Indian thin crepe made with fermented rice and lentils. This is a recipe you need to plan ahead for as there is some overnight soaking involved but no extra work on your part.

> *1 cup basmati rice*
> *1 cup split yellow mung beans (or red lentils if you don't have yellow mung beans in your pantry)*
> *1 ¼ cup water*
> *½ tsp salt*
> *½ tsp coriander powder*
> *Oil for frying*

Rinse rice and mung beans until the water runs clear. Transfer rice and beans into a mixing bowl and cover them with fresh water. Soak overnight. After the soaking period, rinse the mixture. Using a blender, grind the rice and mung beans with the water. (Depending on the size of your blender/food processor, you may have to process the recipe in two batches). Return the batter to a bowl, cover with a towel, and let it ferment for 8 to 12 hours in a warm place.
Cook the dosa as you would cook a pancake, in a frying pan with some oil, butter, or ghee.

Crêpes

Crêpes are to the French what pancakes are to Americans. They actually are quite similar. Crepes are only thinner pancakes. We LOVE crepes. We have them regularly at our house and they usually are the base for a whole meal. We start with savory ones with cheese, béchamel (see recipe p.215) and vegetables toppings and then dessert with some sweet ones garnished with jam, sugar and lemon juice, or chocolate spread.

1 ½ cup flour

1 ½ cup milk

3 tbsp water

3 eggs

1 tbsp sugar

4 tbsp oil

½ tsp salt

Orange blossom water, or Rum (optional)

In a large mixing bowl, whisk together flour, milk, and water until you have a smooth batter. Add eggs, sugar, salt, and any flavoring if you choose to. Mix well. Add butter or oil. Mix again until smooth. Let the batter rest for 30 minutes to 1 hour. (To skip this step, you may want to use warm milk). Heat a lightly oiled griddle or frying pan over medium high heat. Pour or scoop the batter onto the griddle, using approximately 1/4 cup for each crêpe. Tilt the pan with a circular motion so that the batter coats the surface evenly. Cook the crêpe for about 1 minute, until the bottom is light brown. Loosen with a spatula, turn, and cook the other side. Serve hot.

Crêpe Charolaise

This type of crêpe is the oven version of the more traditional crêpe. Perfect for a quick savory meal with a green salad on the side.

1 cup all-purpose flour

3 eggs

¼ tsp salt

1 ¼ cup milk

3 tbsp butter

Toppings: chives, ham, mushrooms, or cheese

Preheat the oven at 425° F. In a bowl, mix all the ingredients together. Pour the batter in a greased cast iron pan or any greased shallow oven safe dish. Add the toppings. Bake for 25 minutes.

Buckwheat Crêpe

This crêpe batter is a classic recipe from Brittany in France. We mostly use it for savory crêpes, with gruyere, ham, egg and mushrooms as toppings. We call them Galettes Bretonnes. The only issue you might have with that recipe is that buckwheat is a gluten-free flour, which means that, on its own, it creates a batter that's very hard to work with. With no gluten, you don't have very much elasticity, leading to friable crêpes. Don't get discouraged if your first crêpes don't turn out great.

2 ¾ cup buckwheat flour

2 tsp salt

3 cups water

1 egg

Mix together the ingredients for the batter either by hand with a whisk or with a blender. Ideally, chill the mixture, covered, at least 30 minutes. When ready to use, stir the batter well. The consistency should be similar to heavy cream (double cream) - if it is too thick add a little water. Warm a crêpe pan or large skillet/frying pan (approx. 12in/30cm diameter) over a medium-high heat. Pour ¼ cup of the crêpe mixture into the warm frying pan/skillet

Breakfast Ideas: Start Your Day Off Right

Let me just say that packaged sugary breakfast cereals are not your only option for your first meal of the day. Breakfast literally means breaking the fast from the night before. It is an important meal as it sets the tone for your day. Over the years, and since our expatriation, I realized a couple of things:

I now consider breakfast as a "real meal." When I was a kid in France, my two favorite times of the day were breakfast and the goûter (the 4pm snack). What did they have in common? We were allowed to eat only sweet stuff (cereals with milk, a piece of baguette with butter and jam, a glass of fresh orange juice, cakes...)

Witnessing my American friends eating salted food for breakfast was such a big eye opener. Why not have some quinoa, scrambled egg, kale, and sausage for breakfast? I feel much better when I don't eat only sweet things at the start of the day.

I don't have to eat first thing in the morning if I don't feel like eating. I will drink some lukewarm water and tea. Most of the time, I will eat later in the morning. I don't force myself to eat just to respect the saying that you can't leave the house on an empty stomach. And if I do, I will always bring along some healthy snacks with me.

The recipes in this section are more on the sweet side but know that you can eat whatever you feel like eating, as long as it is good for your body. Just treat breakfast the same way you consider the other meals of the day. Also, smoothies can be a very good option to break the fast. Go to the self-care section to see some recipe

Pancakes

Since I grew up making crepes all the time, I never really got into pancakes, until we moved to the U.S. However, it is so easy to put together a quick batch for our weekend breakfast. I offer three different versions. Feel free to add fruits, or chocolate chips, to the batter, before you cook them.

Basic Pancakes

1 ½ cup all-purpose flour

1 tbsp baking powder (recipe p.225)

1 tbsp sugar

1 tsp salt

1 ¼ cup milk or buttermilk (see recipe p.224)

1 egg

3 tbsp butter, melted

Quinoa Pancakes

1 cup all-purpose flour

1 cup cooked quinoa

2 tsp baking powder (recipe p.225)

½ tsp baking soda

½ tsp salt

1 egg

1 ¼ cup buttermilk (see recipe p.224)

1 tsp vanilla extract

2 tbsp butter or oil

Gluten-Free Pancakes

2 cups almond flour

½ cup tapioca flour

⅛ tsp salt

1 tbsp baking powder (recipe p.225)

¾ cup almond milk

3 eggs

1 tsp vanilla extract

¼ cup maple syrup

In a large bowl, mix together all the dry ingredients: flour(s), salt, baking powder. Make a well in the center and pour the wet ingredients: milk, egg, vanilla extract, and maple syrup. Mix until smooth. Heat a lightly oiled griddle and use ¼ cup batter for each pancake.

Waffles

I love waffles. I remember when I was a kid, my mom would sometimes surprise my brother and I with some waffles for dinner on a Sunday. She was using her grandma's recipe with a lot of butter. And she always added a drop or two of orange blossom to the batter. They were so delicious!

1 ¾ cup all-purpose flour

½ cup rolled oats

1 tbsp baking powder (recipe p.225)

¼ tsp salt

2 eggs

2 cups milk or buttermilk (see recipe p.224)

2 tbsp olive oil or melted butter

Vanilla extract or orange blossom (optional)

Mix dry ingredients together: flour, oats, baking powder, and salt. Add wet ingredients: eggs, milk, olive oil (or butter). Mix well.

French Toast

French toast is delicious and so easy to make. Here is a fun fact: In France, French toast is called "pain perdu" (lost bread). We usually make this recipe when we have stale bread. I didn't grow up in a house where the bread gets stale, so I discovered French toast when we moved to the U.S. My daughters love these two recipes.

French Toast (with dairy)

1 egg yolk

½ cup cream

½ cup milk

cinnamon, sugar, vanilla extract (optional)

8 slices of bread or brioche

French Toast (dairy free)

1 egg yolk

1 cup of almond milk

2 tbsp almond meal

cinnamon, sugar, vanilla extract (optional)

8 slices of bread or brioche

In a bowl, whisk together eggs, milk, and cinnamon. Pour into a shallow container such as a pie plate. Dip bread in egg mixture. Fry slices until golden brown, then flip to cook the other side. Serve with syrup or powdered sugar.

Granola

Granola was definitely not part of my childhood. Actually, I don't even remember seeing oats in our pantry. I discovered granola when we moved to the U.S. in 2010. And I am so glad I did. Thanks to my Durhamite friend Abby, I learned how easy it is to make your own batch of this delicious and nutritious treat. It's much cheaper than store-bought, naturally sweetened, and so flavorful! You can easily bring in your own twist depending on the season or what you have in your pantry. Don't hesitate to double or triple the recipe. It never lasts long in our house.

Note: Oats are gluten-free by nature, but most are held in facilities that contain gluten. Check the package label if you are concerned with any gluten content.

Note: Did you know that you can make fried granola in less than 10 minutes using the stove? I got this idea from my daughter Abigaëlle who didn't want to use the oven. She divided the recipe in half and made it work beautifully.

Note: Nuts in a granola. I like to roast nuts before adding them to the oats. My daughters don't like it when they are too big. So, I usually use the bottom of a heavy glass and roughly crush the nuts.

Basic Granola Recipe

4 cups rolled oats

½ tsp salt

1 stick melted butter or ½ cup coconut oil

½ cup maple syrup or honey

1 tsp vanilla extract

Then, depending on the flavor we are craving, I add spices, nuts, seeds, and/or dried fruits.

Spices: cinnamon, ginger, nutmeg, pumpkin spices

Nuts: almonds, pistachios, hazelnuts, walnuts, cashews

Seeds: pumpkin, sunflower, sesame, hemp seeds

Dried fruits: cranberries, blueberries, cherries, apricots, crystallized ginger, apples.

Different flavor combinations of spices and nuts for granola;

Apple Pie Granola

1-2 cups of a mix chopped nuts

½ shredded coconut (optional)

1 to 2 tsp cinnamon

½ tsp ginger

¼ tsp cardamom

1 cup dried apples

Lemon Blueberry Granola

1-2 cups of a mix chopped nuts

Juice of 2 lemons (about ½ cup)

1 cup dried blueberries

½ cup shredded coconut

Peanut Butter Chocolate Chip Granola

1-2 cups of a mix of chopped nuts

½ cup melted peanut butter

¾ cup chocolate chips

½ cup raisins (optional)

Preheat the oven to 350° F. I like to use that time of preheating to melt the wet ingredients (butter, coconut oil, peanut butter ....) placing them in an oven-proof container. If I feel like it, I will also roast the chopped nuts during that time to give an extra kick of flavor. If not, I just add them directly to the mix. Line a baking sheet with parchment paper and set aside (or grease the baking sheet). In a bowl, combine rolled oats, chopped nuts, spices, and salt into a bowl and mix thoroughly. Add the wet ingredients: maple syrup or honey, butter or coconut oil, vanilla extract, lemon juice (if you choose to make the lemon blueberry version), peanut butter (for the PB / chocolate chips version). Mix well to coat everything. Transfer mixture onto the baking sheet. Bake at 350° F for 22 to 25 minutes, stirring once at 12 minutes. If you like your granola on the crunchier side, you can cook it longer. Also, if you like big clusters, don't stir it as often. Remove from the oven and let cool for at least 30 minutes and up to overnight. Once cool, add chocolate chips or dried fruits depending on the recipe chosen.

Gluten-Free, Dairy Free, and Sugar-Free Banana Bread (or Muffins)

I love this recipe so much! The riper the bananas, the better the cake will turn out. Don't be afraid of using very brown bananas. It's a good recipe when you have to please a crowd with dairy or gluten sensitivities.

> *4 ripe bananas*
> *3 eggs*
> *½ cup almond butter or peanut butter*
> *½ cup coconut flour, almond flour, or oat flour*
> *1 tsp baking powder (see recipe p.225)*
> *1 tsp vanilla extract*
> *Pinch of salt*
> *1 tsp cinnamon (optional)*

Preheat the oven to 350°F. In a bowl, mash the bananas with a fork until completely smooth. Mix in the eggs, and the peanut or almond butter. Add all the dry ingredients: flour, baking powder and salt and spices. Mix well and pour the batter in a greased loaf pan. Bake for 55 minutes to 1 hour. Remove from the oven and let cool in the pan for a few minutes. Then remove the banana bread from the pan and let cool completely before serving.

Gluten-Free Apple Blueberry Muffins

One of my favorite gluten-free treats. I often add some diced apples to the batter and reduce the sugar, and they always turn out great. This recipe is very forgiving. Feel free to substitute starch or gluten free flour with what you have available.

> *½ cup almond flour*

½ cup tapioca starch or cornstarch

½ cup brown rice flour (or any other gluten free flour)

½ cup sugar

1 tsp baking powder (see recipe p.225)

½ tsp salt

1 tsp vanilla extract

3 eggs

½ cup olive oil (or any other oils)

1 cup blueberry

1 apple, peeled and finely diced (optional)

Preheat the oven to 375° F. Mix all the dry ingredients: flour, baking powder, salt, and sugar. Add beaten eggs, olive oil, and vanilla extract. Mix well. Add the blueberries (and apple) and stir gently. Pour the batter into muffins tins (silicone or paper ones). Bake for 25 minutes. If you want a loaf, use a 5-inch x 9-inch x 3-inch loaf dish. Bake for about 55 minutes.

Lunch Ideas: Grab and Go

Lunch is the meal of the day that can be easily skipped as we get ourselves too busy. Unfortunately, if we don't make time to take at least 20 minutes to pause, sit, and eat, we will pay for it later in the day, snacking on the first thing we can find, totally ruled by our cravings. With a touch of mindfulness and planning, you can change this bad habit and set yourself up for a successful rest of your day. The night before, make a plan for what you will eat for lunch the next day. It can be leftovers, a quick salad fix, or a sandwich. I don't care what you pick but make a plan.

QUICHES, SAVORY PIES, AND CAKES

Quiche

A quiche is a savory egg custard baked in a pie crust. The base of the filling is a combination of eggs, cream, and milk. The add-ins vary and can include meat, seafood, vegetables, cheese, and spices. I love this dish because it is so versatile. You can easily make a whole meal with it by adding a nice salad as a side dish. It is also a perfect format for a potluck, a picnic, or when you are on the go. I make quiches all year round playing with the vegetables that are in season.

1 savory pie crust or Olive oil Tart Dough (see recipe p.236 and p.237)

Filling

>*4 eggs*
>
>*½ cup milk*
>
>*½ cup heavy cream (if you don't have heavy cream on hand, replace with 1 cup of milk)*

Add-ins

>*2 cups of vegetables (asparagus, broccoli, kale, spinach, leeks, bell peppers, mushrooms, or onions...)*
>
>*½ to 1 cup of cheese (mozzarella, parmesan, Swiss, or goat cheese...)*

Optional: Meat or seafood (bacon, ham, chicken, salmon, tuna...)

Spread the pie crust in a pan. Poke holes with a fork all over the crust and put it in the fridge. Preheat the oven to 375° F. Whisk eggs and milk/cream in a bowl. Pre-cook the vegetables you want to add in: Sauté mushroom, or leeks, spinach. Cover the bottom of the pie crust with Dijon mustard. Spread vegetables, cheese, and meat/seafood evenly on the crust and then pour the egg mixture on top. Bake until the filling is set, between 40mn and 50mn. Let cool at least 20mn before slicing.

Add-in combination suggestions:
- The most popular is Quiche Lorraine with bacon/ham and cheese.
- Sautéed chopped leeks + smoked salmon + dill (fresh or dried)
- Spinach, tomatoes, goat cheese
- Broccoli and red onion
- Roasted pepper, scallion and sausage

Tarte à la Tomate (Tomato Tart)

My daughters like to call this dish "Pizza pie." It is a staple in our family during summertime when tomatoes are so abundant and flavorful. It is a perfect lunch idea for a light summer bite, paired with a salad.

1 savory pie crust (see recipe p.236 and p.237)
1 tbsp Dijon mustard
4 to 5 tomatoes, sliced
10 Slices of fresh mozzarella cheese or gruyere cheese (optional)
Herbs of Provence or oregano

Preheat the oven to 375° F. Fit the pie crust into a 9-inch pie dish. With a fork, poke holes into the bottom of the crust. Spread the mustard over the bottom of the pie crust in an even layer. Arrange slices of tomatoes (and cheese if you choose to), overlapping in a spiral from the edge to the center. Sprinkle the tart with the herbs of Provence. Bake in the preheated oven until the crust has browned, and the tomatoes are curled at the edges, about 20 minutes.

French Savory Cake (cake salé)

Cake salé is a staple in France. It is an easy dish to bring at a picnic or for a potluck.

2½ cup all-purpose flour, plus more for the pan
2 tsp baking powder (recipe p.225)
1 tsp fine sea salt
½ tsp baking soda
4 tbsp butter, melted and cooled, plus more for the pan
2 large eggs
1 cup buttermilk or milk
1 cup coarsely chopped ham
3 tbsp thinly sliced scallions, white and green parts (optional)
1 tbsp chopped fresh thyme leaves
2 cups grated Gruyere or sharp cheddar cheese

Heat the oven to 350° F. Butter and flour a 9 × 5-inch loaf pan and set it aside. In a large bowl, whisk together the flour, baking powder, salt, and baking soda. Add the melted butter, eggs, and buttermilk. Whisk well to combine. Stir in the chopped ham, scallions if using, thyme, and 1¾ cups of the Gruyere (reserving the rest for topping). Transfer the batter to the prepared loaf pan and spread it out evenly, smoothing the top. Sprinkle the remaining ¼ cup (1 ounce) cheese over the top. Bake for 45 to 55 minutes, until a skewer inserted in the center comes out with some moist crumbs attached. Transfer the pan to a wire rack and let it cool for 10 minutes. Then remove the bread from the pan and let it cool completely on the wire rack.

Combination ideas for filling:

- bacon, mushroom, olives
- oregano, hot sauce, dried tomatoes, two fresh tomatoes
- can of tuna, zucchinis, whipping cream or sour cream

SANDWICHES AND SPREADS

Croque monsieur (Grilled cheese sandwich)

I remember vividly every Sunday night our family made Croque-Monsieur for dinner. They are the French version of the grilled sandwich, made with ham, Gruyere cheese, and occasionally béchamel sauce on top. It was such a fun tradition for me. It lasted for years. I was in the kitchen with my dad slicing some cheese and assembling the sandwiches, before baking them in a special machine that belonged to my grandmother.

Makes 4 Croque Monsieur sandwiches

1 tsp Dijon mustard

8 slices of bread

8 oz Gruyere cheese (or any cheese), sliced

8 thick slices of ham

Béchamel sauce (optional)

Turn on the oven's broil setting. * Spread Dijon mustard over half of the bread slices. Top half of the bread slices with cheese, and 2 slices of ham each. Then top the ham with more cheese. Place the remaining bread slices to assemble the sandwiches. Spread about 1-2 tbsp bechamel sauce over the top of each sandwich. Add some more shredded cheese on top of the bechamel. Set the sandwiches on a baking sheet on the middle rack of your oven until the cheese is beginning to melt and bubble. Move the sandwiches to the top rack for about 30 seconds, keeping your eye on it and removing when the cheese starts to obtain little golden spots.

* If you don't want to use your oven, just cook the sandwiches in a pan. Just add the béchamel after flipping the sandwich to cook the other side.

Note: A croque monsieur served with a poached or lightly fried egg on top is known as a croque madame.

Veggie Burgers (or veggie patties)

When my daughters were toddlers, I started blending some oats with vegetables (broccoli, onions, carrots, celery…), eggs, and a little bit of milk. I baked that mixture in the oven and got some healthy snacks on the go. Since then, I have been using the same base to do vegetable patties. They are perfect for veggie burgers! I like to use a round cookie cutter to shape the patties. There is room for improvisation. You can use any vegetables available in your fridge (carrots, kale, spinach, broccoli, turnips, peppers, green onions, or mushrooms). And of course, season with your favorite spices! They freeze very well and can also be use as crumbs for salads.

1 cup oats

2 cup vegetables, chopped

½ cup flaxseed meal or breadcrumbs for binding agent

pinch of salt

1 tbsp mustard (optional)

spices to your taste (curry, cumin, chili powder…)

Preheat the oven at 375° F. In a food processor, add oats, vegetables, flaxseed or breadcrumbs, and salt. Blend until you obtain a mixture. Add spices and mustard. Use a baking sheet with a piece of parchment on and form the patties with a round cookie cutter or the top of a glass. Brush the patties with some butter, oil, or ghee. Bake the patties in the oven for about 20 minutes, flipping them halfway. The patties are ready to serve. They are good for a couple of days, stored in the fridge. Just reheat them on a pan to make them crispy.

No-Mayo Tuna Spread

I have never been a big fan of mayonnaise. This tuna spread recipe doesn't use mayo but instead avocado. It is quick and easy to make. Plus, it is very flavorful. Feel free to add different herbs and spices you have on hand (diced onions, cilantro....). You can use it as a spread or as a salad.

> *1 can tuna (5 ounces)*
> *1 small/medium avocado*
> *1 carrot, chopped or grated*
> *1 celery stalk, finely chopped*
> *2 tbsp lemon or lime juice*
> *1 tsp dried dill*
> *1 tsp smoked paprika*
> *½ tsp salt*

In a medium bowl, mash together the tuna and avocado. Add the remaining ingredients and mix well. Serve in a sandwich or over a bed of lettuce.

Salmon Spread

This spread is easy to put together and perfect when slathered on crackers, crusty bread, or with vegetables as a dip.

> *1 can salmon*
> *1 slice smoked salmon (optional)*
> *2 green onions, mostly the white parts*
> *2 celery stalks, finely chopped*
> *1 tsp dill*
> *2 tsp lemon juice*
> *1 tbsp Greek yogurt*
> *Salt and pepper*

In a medium bowl, mash together salmon, green onions, celery and dill. Add the dill, lemon juice, Greek yogurt and mix well. Serve in a sandwich or over a bed of lettuce.

SOUPS ON THE GO

I highly recommend investing in some thermos containers so you can bring a warm meal wherever you go. They are perfect for soups and stews on the go. Put a bunch of fresh ingredients and seasonings in a mason jar or any closed container. Carry some hot water (or chicken/vegetable broth) with you, and when you are ready to eat, pour the warm liquid over the ingredients. You have an instant, healthy soup on the go. Perfect for a quick lunch or when you go camping. Thank you for Gwyneth Paltrow's cookbooks for the inspiration!

Black Bean Soup

    ½ cup black beans

    2 tsp tomato paste

    ½ tsp chili powder

    ½ tsp cumin

    3 tbsp corn (can be frozen)

    ⅓ cup spiralized zucchinis

    Cilantro, lime juice, to taste

    Salt or homemade bouillon paste (see recipe p. 207)

Thai Curry Noodle Soup

    ½ cup cooked soba noodles

    1 tbsp soy sauce

    ½ tsp curry paste

    1 tsp coconut oil or sesame oil

    2 tbsp coconut milk

½ tsp grated ginger

2 mushrooms (shiitake, white button)

Salt or homemade bouillon paste (see recipe p.207)

ONE BOWL MEALS

Poke Bowl

Sushi is our love language in our family. But making your own sushi can be time consuming and quite a technical challenge. That's why I love poke bowls so much. It is quick, easy to assemble, and completely addicting! Traditional poke is made with tuna or some kind of fish. For this version, we use marinated tofu. I adapted the recipe from the blog, Simple Veganista.

>   14 oz block organic tofu (firm or extra firm), cut into 1/2-inch cubes*
>   Lime soy ginger marinade (see recipe p.221)
>   ½ cucumber, sliced
>   1 cup carrot, shredded
>   ¼ red cabbage, shredded (optional but gives a nice color)
>   1 avocado, diced
>   2 scallions, white and green parts, sliced thinly on the bias
>   Nori sheet, cut into strips
>   Pickled ginger (optional)
>   Sesame seeds to garnish
>   2 cups cooked rice (sushi, brown or white rice) **
>   Sauce: mix 1 tbsp soy sauce with 1 tbsp maple syrup.

Drain the tofu and place it on its side, cut in half down the long side. Place on a clean dish cloth or between paper towels and gently press to soak up some of the moisture. Dice the tofu into ½-inch cubes. In a medium bowl or shallow dish, toss in the tofu with the marinade and let rest in for 10 minutes. Prep the remaining ingredients and assemble your bowls.

*If you enjoy some seafood, you can replace tofu with sushi grade salmon, or tuna. Smoked salmon works great too.
**I like to use seasoned sushi rice. I use the Instant Pot® to prepare it: Rinse 2 cups of sushi rice very well. Transfer it to the Instant Pot® with 2 cups of water. Set up the Instant Pot® on low pressure for 12 minutes. Allow a natural pressure release for 10 minutes. While the rice is cooking, I prepare the seasoning. In a bowl, add ½ cup rice vinegar, 1 ½ teaspoon salt, and 2 tablespoons sugar. Mix well and add it to the cooked rice, stirring thoroughly.

Buddha Bowls

A Buddha bowl is a one-dish meal consisting of grains, leafy greens, roasted or raw veggies, a source of proteins and a light drizzle of dressing. This is really THE dish that is made for improvisation and customization based on what you have on hand and what combination of ingredients you like. Keep it colorful and filled with different textures to get the most nutrients.

Choose Grains

Quinoa, barley, brown rice, couscous, cauliflower rice, or any other whole grain you enjoy can be used! There really are no rules.

Top with Greens and Veggies

 Lay a bed of spinach, lettuce, kale, or arugula on top of the grains. Top with roasted sweet potato, butternut squash, fresh tomato, peppers, or avocado. Use any leftover veggies from the fridge or whatever vegetable you love most.

Pile on the protein

falafels, beans, roasted chickpeas, lentils, soft-boiled egg, chicken, tuna, salmon, or crispy tofu

Add Garnishes
Top it with nuts, seeds, and/or cheese. Sesame seeds, sunflower seeds, pumpkin seeds, walnuts, pecans, almonds, cashews, pine nuts or pistachios would all work well. You can also sprinkle on feta, or another crumble cheese like gorgonzola, goat, or blue cheese.

Dressing(see section homemade staple p)
vinaigrette, tzatziki sauce, cashew sauce...

CHOPPED SALADS

There is no better weekday meal than a protein-packed chopped salad. The flavor combinations are endless. They are pretty cheap and so easy to put together. If you eat them at home, mix all the ingredients in a bowl. And if you pack them to go, arrange them so the ingredients stay separate and pack dressing on the side. That way, nothing gets soggy.

Quinoa, Kale, and Black Bean Salad
This salad is my favorite quick meal. A perfect candidate for a make-ahead salad. It even tastes better the next day. It is also a great side dish to bring to a potluck. Plus, it is cost effective and very flavorful.

1/4 cup extra virgin olive oil
1 tsp ground cumin
1 clove garlic, pressed, grated or finely chopped
Juice of one lime (about 2 tbsp)

1 tsp salt or homemade bouillon paste, to taste (see recipe p. 207)

¼ tsp cayenne pepper (optional for heat)

1 small bunch of curly green or Tuscan kale, chopped into small pieces (or about 3 cups roughly chopped baby spinach)

One 15-ounce can black beans, rinsed and drained well

2 cups cooked quinoa (1 cup dry quinoa yields about 2 cups cooked)

1 red bell pepper, chopped (about 1 cup)

1 small red onion, chopped

1 handful cilantro, roughly chopped (about ⅓ cup)

Optional: corn, crumbled feta cheese, pumpkin seeds...

Whisk the olive oil, cumin, garlic, lime, salt, and cayenne pepper together in the bottom of a large bowl. Add the chopped kale, massaging it with your hands until the kale gets darker and more fragrant (it makes it easier to eat). Rinse and drain the black beans. Chop the veggies until roughly the same size as the black beans. Add in black beans, chopped veggies, and cooked quinoa to the bowl and mix until all the ingredients are well combined.

Mediterranean Lentil Salad

This healthy salad is make-ahead friendly and perfect for weekday lunches. It is sure to satisfy.

1 cup dried brown lentils

4 cups water or vegetable broth (see recipe p.209)

1 tsp salt or homemade bouillon paste, to taste (see recipe p. 207)

1 small red onion, chopped

1 cucumber, diced

3 tomatoes, diced

⅓ cup fresh parsley, chopped

⅓ cup crumbled feta cheese, or mozzarella cheese

¼ cup balsamic vinaigrette

In a large saucepan, combine the lentils and water or broth. Bring to a boil over medium high heat and then turn to low and cook for 20 to 25 minutes or until lentils are soft, but still slightly firm. Do not overcook or the lentils will be mushy. When the lentils are done cooking, use a colander to drain the lentils. Discard the bay leaf. Rinse quickly with cold water. Transfer to a large bowl. Add the cucumber, red pepper, red onion, parsley, mint, and feta cheese, if using, to the bowl and stir. Drizzle with dressing and toss until well combined. Serve immediately or let sit for 30 minutes so the flavors can meld.

Dinner Ideas:
At the Dinner Table

For our family, the only time of the day we are together at home is around dinnertime. We try to make it a moment of connection and checking in with one another, over a simple meal.

PLANT-BASED DISHES

Vegetable tian (lazier version of ratatouille)

Ratatouille is a classic end-of-summer French stew, packed with fresh produce: tomatoes, eggplant, zucchini, yellow squash, and bell peppers. In Provence (where I grew up), ratatouille is typically cooked on the stove. But it can be tricky to prepare as this dish combines vegetables that have different cook times. That's why I prefer his cousin dish: Vegetable tian. Same ingredients but everything is put together in layers and cooked in the oven.

> *1 large onion*
> *3 garlic cloves*
> *1 large eggplant, sliced*
> *4 large tomatoes, sliced*
> *3 or 4 medium size zucchinis, sliced*
> *3 sweet bell peppers, sliced (optional)*
> *½ tsp salt or 1 tsp homemade bouillon paste, to taste (see recipe p. 207)*
> *Oregano or Italian seasoning to sprinkle on top*

Note: Sometimes I like to add layers of cooked rice or cooked quinoa, cheese, and ham to make it a complete meal.

Preheat the oven to 375° F. Slice the vegetables into ¼" thick slices. I prefer to chop the onions finely and sauté them with garlic and olive oil, but you can also just slice them like the other vegetables. Layer the vegetables in a greased dish. Drizzle with a tablespoon of olive oil and sprinkle with herbs, salt, and pepper. Cover tightly with foil and bake for 45 minutes. Remove the foil, sprinkle with cheese, and bake for an additional 20 minutes, until browned.

Gratin Dauphinois (scalloped potatoes)

Gratin dauphinois is named after the Dauphiné region of France. It is a combination of potatoes soaked with garlic-infused cream slow-cooked to melting perfection. It is about as good as it gets when it comes to comfort food. The original recipe isn't topped with cheese, but I know that many families like to add some Swiss cheese or mozzarella to make it even more decadent. It takes a little time and effort to peel and then slice potatoes, but it is worth it! I like to use a mandolin to slice the potatoes. Doing so, this guarantees similar size cuts for even baking.

1 cup whole milk

1 cup heavy cream

1 tsp salt or homemade bouillon paste, to taste (see recipe p. 207)

½ tsp nutmeg (or more to your taste)

3 pounds baking potatoes, peeled and cut crosswise into 1/4-inch slices (Yukon gold potatoes are my favorite) *

4 garlic cloves, finely chopped

Preheat the oven at 410°F. In a bowl, mix milk, cream, garlic cloves, salt, and nutmeg. Butter a large baking dish and layer the potatoes. Cover with the cream mixture. Bake in the oven for 50 minutes.

*Keep the potato peels to make delicious crispy potato skin chips. To do so, pre-heat the oven at 350°F. In a bowl, massage the potato peels with some olive oil. Transfer the potato peels on a baking sheet. Sprinkle them with some salt. Place in the oven and bake for 15 minutes or until you obtain crispy golden chips. You may need to stay close to the oven to check regularly.

Falafels Patties

Falafel is a popular Middle Eastern "fast food" made with chickpeas. Traditionally, it is deep fried to yield a crispy texture. It is often served in a pita bread with tahini sauce or hummus, along with a tomato and cucumber salad.

Version with Chickpea Flour
- *1 cup garbanzo flour (chickpea flour)*
- *½ tsp salt*
- *1 tsp baking powder (see recipe p.225)*
- *½ tsp cumin*
- *½ tsp coriander*
- *2 garlic cloves (or 1 tsp garlic powder)*
- *1 small, chopped onion (or 1 tsp onion powder)*
- *Juice of 1 lemon*
- *½ cup warm water or broth (see recipe p.209)*
- *1 cup fresh herbs (parsley, cilantro, dill…)*

Combine all the dry ingredients in a bowl and blend thoroughly. Add the lemon juice and hot water to the dry ingredients and stir until combined. Let the mixture rest for 10 minutes.

Version with Canned Chickpeas:
- *3 (size of can) canned chickpeas*
- *4 garlic cloves*
- *1 small onion, coarsely chopped or 4 scallions, thinly sliced*
- *1 cup fresh herbs (cilantro, parsley…)*
- *1 ½ tsp salt*
- *1 tsp cumin*
- *1 tsp coriander*

1 tsp baking powder (see recipe p.225)
1/3 cup chickpea flour or all-purpose flour

In a frying pan, heat oil on medium-high heat until hot. Add the falafel batter by the tablespoon and flatten slightly. Fry on both sides until golden brown. Place on a paper towel to drain oil. If you prefer, you can bake the falafel patties in a 350° F heated oven for about 15-20 minutes, turning them over midway through. Use a lightly oiled sheet pan and give the patties a quick brush of extra virgin olive oil before baking.

Tip to Make-Ahead: Prepare the falafel mixture and divide into patties. Place the patties on a baking sheet, lined and then freeze. When they harden, you can transfer the falafel patties into a freezer bag. They will keep well in the freezer for a month or so. You can fry or bake them frozen.

Red Lentil Curry with Coconut Rice

Easiest recipe ever. But nourishing and flavorful. When I don't know what to eat but need something quick and filling, this is my go-to meal. It is a crowd pleaser, especially with kids. A must-have in your meal rotation.

1 red lentils coulis recipe (see p.219)
2 cups roasted veggies of your choice
2 cups white rice
2 cups coconut milk

Add water, spices, butter and lentils in a pot. Bring it to boil and simmer until the water has almost completely evaporated.
Note: You can add diced onions, cilantro, diced carrots, or spinach...

To make the coconut rice, simply replace the water to cook the rice with coconut milk. Start by rinsing your rice several times, until the water turns clear.

If I use the Instant Pot®, I add 2 cups rice for 2 cups coconut milk and pressure cook for 7 minutes.

If using the stovetop, I add the same ratio of rice and coconut milk and cook until the coconut milk is absorbed by the rice.

Pour the coulis over the rice and roasted veggies.

Dairy-Free Mac and Cheese

Mac and cheese is not a staple food in France, but the closest equivalent would be "timbale de macaronis." It is a pasta dish made with pieces of ham with bechamel sauce, topped with cheese and breadcrumbs. This flavorful version below is filled with vegetables and healthy fats.

> *Orange sauce (see recipe p.218)*
> *Breadcrumbs, cheese (optional)*
> *One 16 oz package pasta*

In a pot, add onion, carrots, potatoes, celery, and water. Bring it to a boil. Cover the pan and simmer for 15mn or until the vegetables are soft. Transfer the vegetables with the water in a blender. Add the rest of the ingredients and blend until smooth. Cook pasta according to the package instructions to have them al-dente. Preheat the oven to 350° F. Mix cooked pasta and sauce and transfer them in an oven-safe dish. Top it with breadcrumbs and cheese if you feel like it. Bake for 20 minutes.

Sweet Potatoes, Black Beans, and Quinoa Burgers

One of my four daughters is a vegetarian, and this veggie burger recipe is her favorite.

> *2 14oz canned black beans*
> *2 sweet potatoes, cooked*
> *1 cup quinoa, cooked*
> *1 small onion, chopped*

4 garlic cloves

Salt or homemade bouillon paste, to taste (see recipe p.207)

½ cup fresh finely chopped cilantro

½ cup breadcrumbs (optional)

Place all the ingredients in a food processor and blend for a few seconds. Use a baking sheet with a piece of parchment on and form the patties with a round cookie cutter or the top of a glass. Brush the patties with some butter, oil, or ghee. Bake the patties for about 20 minutes, flipping them halfway. Those veggie burgers are good for a couple of days, stored in the fridge. Just reheat them on a pan to make them crispy. They also freeze very well.

Easy Burrito Pot (Instant Pot®)

Thanks to Lisa Burns in her cookbook Family Meals from Scratch in your Instant Pot®, I realized that it was possible to cook beans and rice all together in a pressure cooker. Her recipe revolutionized our Tex-mex nights at home. From this magic pot, you will be able to make delicious burritos, nachos, quesadillas, tacos in no time! Here is my version of this Easy Burrito Pot.

1 cup short grain brown rice

1 cup dried black beans

3 ½ cups water or broth (see recipe p.209)

1 tsp oregano

1 tsp ground cumin

½ tsp garlic powder

½ tsp onion powder

½ tsp chili powder*

2 tsp salt or homemade bouillon paste, to taste (recipe p.207)

* *You can replace all the spices above with 1 tbsp Mexican blend spice (see recipe p.205)*

Combine and stir water with rice, beans, and spices in your Instant Pot®. Place the lid on the Instant Pot® and turn the valve to Sealing. Set the cooking time for 40 minutes on high pressure. When the cook time is complete, let the pressure naturally release. Stir the rice and bean mixture. Decide what you want to enjoy for dinner, adding your favorite fixing.

Note: Because of the high-water content in the pot, the dish will take longer to come to pressure and will release more pressure than other dishes, about 90 minutes total from start to finish.

Bruschetta

Nothing screams summer quite like bruschetta. Bread, fresh tomatoes, basil, and garlic are all you need to make this recipe. It is a delicious toast appetizer. Make it a whole meal with a nice salad on the side.

For the topping

4 large tomatoes, diced

¼ cup thinly sliced basil

2 tbsp balsamic vinegar

4 tbsp olive oil

2 cloves garlic, thinly sliced

1 tsp salt

Pinch of crushed red pepper flakes

Fresh mozzarella, diced (optional)

For the bread

1 large baguette, sliced ¼" thick on the bias

Olive oil, for brushing

2 cloves garlic, halved

In a large bowl, toss together tomatoes, basil, vinegar, olive oil, garlic, salt, and red pepper flakes. Let marinate for at least 30 minutes. Meanwhile, toast bread. Preheat the oven to 400° F. Brush bread on both sides lightly with oil and place on a large baking sheet. Toast bread until golden, 10 to 15 minutes, turning halfway through. Let bread cool for 5 minutes, then rub tops of bread with halved garlic cloves. Spoon marinated tomatoes on top of bread just before serving.

Note: If the tomatoes are too wet, the toast will be soggy. The trick: Salt your tomatoes. After they have been diced, add them to a large strainer or colander over a bowl, and toss with some salt. Let sit for 5 minutes. There will be lots of liquid at the bottom of the bowl. Discard the liquid when you are done. This salting trick also improves the quality of out-of-season tomatoes.

Note: If you prefer to keep your tomato mixture from sliding off the toasted bread, consider a spread before you top them with the mixture. Whipped ricotta or basil pesto both work well.

DISHES WITH ANIMAL PROTEINS

Fish Dish Baked in Foil

The idea of cooking fish can be intimidating. There is a fear of the fish not cooking right or sticking to the pan or grill. And you are often left with the inevitable fishy smell in the house with a dread for cleaning up. We don't eat much fish, maybe once every other week. This foil method is our fish go-to in the kitchen. It doesn't take much planning or time, and cooking is easy and stress-free. It makes for a sublime tasting fish dish and a ridiculously carefree cleanup.

For 4 persons

4 individual fish filets (we like to use cod or salmon)
Marinade of your choice (we used olive oil, a bit of soy sauce, fresh herbs, green onions, and garlic)
4 zucchinis, diced
4 peppers, diced
4 tomatoes, diced
2 onions, diced
4 aluminum foil sheets

Preheat the oven at 375° F*. Dice all the vegetables and mix them together. Place four pieces of aluminum on a baking sheet. On each sheet, lay down a bed of vegetables and add the fish on top. Spoon the marinade on top of the fish. Fold the foil tightly by bringing up all four sides to create a packet around the fish. Pinch each of the four edges, then bring them together to fold and seal the packet closed. Bake until the fish is cooked through, about 15 to 20 minutes, depending upon the type and size of fish.

*If you decide to use the barbecue to cook the fish, place the foil packets directly on the barbecue over medium heat. Cook for 15 to 20 minutes until fish become flaky and fork-tender and vegetables are cooked.

Ceviche

Ceviche is a method of "cooking" seafood by letting it marinate in citrus juices. You can use salmon, tuna, scallops, shrimp, or red snapper. It is a popular dish in Central and South American cuisine. Quick, easy, and no stove required!

> *1 pound fresh or frozen fish cut into ½ inch pieces*
> *⅓ cup lime or lemon juice*
> *1 avocado, diced*
> *1 mango, diced*
> *1 large tomato, diced*
> *½ cup red onion, finely diced*
> *1 jalapeno Chile pepper, seeded and minced (optional)*
> *3 tbsp cilantro, chopped*
> *¼ tsp salt*

In a bowl, combine the fish with lemon juice. Allow to marinate in the refrigerator for 4 to 8 hours, mixing a couple of times during that time. Drain the fish and discard the liquid. Put the fish in a bowl and add the rest of the ingredients. Gently stir to combine.

Fish Cakes

Here is a great recipe for fish cake using canned chickpeas and canned salmon or tuna. Canned seafood is an affordable, shelf-stable option for a quick meal when time or budget doesn't allow for cooking with fresh ingredients.

> *One 14oz can chickpeas, drained and mashed or 1 cup mashed potatoes*
> *1 12oz can wild Alaska salmon or wild-caught tuna, drained*
> *½ cup frozen peas, thawed*
> *1 small bunch green onions, finely chopped*
> *1 egg*

1 tbsp fresh cilantro, dill or mint, finely chopped

½ tsp fresh ginger, chopped (or ¼ tsp ground ginger)

1 tsp salt or homemade bouillon paste (see separate recipe p.207)

⅛ tsp chile flakes

Place chickpeas in a food processor with 2 tbsp olive oil. Blend to roughly puree the chickpeas. (You can also mash the chickpeas using a fork). Place all the ingredients in a large mixing bowl. Stir the ingredients together with a fork, breaking apart the fish, until evenly combined. Portion the mixture into patties (about 2 tablespoons each). Coat the bottom of a large skillet with cooking oil and heat to medium-high. Fry fish cakes in batches until golden brown, about 3 minutes per side. You can also bake the patties in the oven at 375° F for 20mn (flipping the patties halfway).

Pakistani Kima

I love the complex flavor of this comforting one pot meal. It makes the house smell amazing! Original Pakistani Kima is made with white potatoes, but substituting sweet potatoes works just as well. If you want to make this dish vegetarian, you can substitute ground meat with beans or tofu, too.

2 tbsp olive oil or ghee

1 chopped medium onion

2 garlic cloves

1 pound ground beef (any ground meat works well).

1 tbsp curry

2 tsp salt or homemade bouillon paste (see separate recipe p.207)

1 tsp cinnamon

1 tsp ginger

1 tsp turmeric

3 potatoes, diced very small

3 cups fresh diced tomatoes (or 2 cans of diced tomatoes)

2 cups frozen peas

Melt oil in a large pan. Add onion and garlic. Cook until onions soften. Add meat and cook thoroughly. Add curry, salt, and spices. Stir well. Add potatoes and tomatoes to the pan. Bring to a simmering boil. Reduce heat, cover, and cook for about 15 minutes or until the potatoes are done. Add the peas at the end of the cooking time so they keep their vibrant color. Serve alone or over rice or cauliflower rice.

Chakchouka

Chakchouka is an easy and hearty African dish of eggs in a fragrant tomato sauce with vegetables. Quick and easy to make.

2 tbsp olive oil or ghee
1 medium onion, chopped
1 bell pepper, finely sliced
3 garlic cloves, minced
6 medium tomatoes, diced (or 2 14oz cans of diced tomatoes)
1 tsp cumin
1 tsp paprika
½ tsp chili powder
½ tsp salt or homemade bouillon paste, to taste (see recipe p.207)
4 eggs

In a large cast iron skillet or sauté pan, heat oil and cook the onion, until softened. Add the pepper and garlic. Sauté for an additional 3 to 5 minutes. Add the tomatoes, cumin, paprika, salt and chili powder. Mix well and bring the mixture to a simmer. Simmer, uncovered for 10 to 15 minutes until the mixture has thickened. Using the back of a spoon, make 4 craters in the mixture, and crack one egg into each of the craters. Cover the skillet and simmer for 5-7 minutes, until the eggs have set. Serve immediately with crusty bread or pita to dip in.

Chicken or Turkey Lucullus Cutlets

I was first introduced to this dish thanks to my dad. It is one of the rare recipes he liked to make when I was a kid. The Lucullus cutlet requires a piece of meat, bacon, and cheese. One of the Americans' favorite foods, right? This simple French Savoyard specialty is usually served with pasta, green vegetables, or braised endives. It is perfect for evenings with friends. This recipe can be made in the oven or on the stove.

4 chicken breasts, turkey breasts or veal, thinly sliced lengthwise
Salt and pepper
1 tbsp flour
2 tbsp butter or olive oil
Juice of ½ lemon (optional)
4 bacon slices
4 Swiss cheese or any cheese you like
½ cup white wine or broth

Oven version:
Preheat the oven to 320° F. Salt and pepper, and then flour the meat. In a skillet, melt the butter then brown the cutlets on each side (about 2mn per side). Then sprinkle them with lemon juice. Cover each cutlet with a slice of bacon and a slice of cheese. In a baking dish, arrange your cutlets with the cooking sauce and the broth or white wine. Bake for 7 minutes.

Note: For a more gourmet recipe, you can add mushrooms and a spoonful of fresh cream before baking.

Instant Pot® version:
Sauté the floured meat in butter and brown it on both sides. Sprinkle it with lemon juice. Cover each cutlet with a slice of bacon and a slice of cheese. Add broth or wine and close the lid. Set the cooking time for 5 minutes on high pressure.

Butter Chicken (Instant Pot®)

This dish is a crowd pleaser and so easy to make. My 7-year-old daughter was able to make it all by herself! You just pour all the ingredients in the Instant Pot®, and voilà!

1 14.5oz can tomato sauce or can crushed/diced tomatoes

6 garlic cloves

1 tbsp minced ginger

2 tsp garam masala

1 tsp turmeric

1 tsp paprika

1 tsp cumin

¼ tsp cayenne pepper

1 tsp salt or 1tbsp homemade bouillon paste (see recipe p.207)

1 pound boneless and skinless chicken breasts or thighs, cut into bite-size pieces

1 stick butter or ½ cup coconut oil

½ cup coconut milk

½ cup cilantro, chopped

Add all spices, tomato sauce, and chicken in the Instant Pot®. Set the cooking time for 10 minutes on high pressure. Add butter, coconut milk, and cilantro. Enjoy over a bowl of rice. Note: If you don't have a pressure cooker, marinate the chicken with all the spices, garlic, and salt. Heat oil in a large skillet or pot over medium-high heat. Place chicken in the pan and cook for around 3 minutes, or until the chicken is white all over. Add the crushed tomatoes. Turn the heat down to low and simmer for 20 minutes. Add butter, coconut milk and cilantro.

Stuffed Baked Tomatoes with Rice

One pan dish from my childhood that is easy, flavorful, and colorful. These baked stuffed tomatoes cooked on a bed of rice are a great family dish. It can easily be prepared ahead of time.

4 to 6 large tomatoes
Salt
1 onion, minced
2 garlic cloves, minced
1 slice of bread, turned into crumbs
2 tsp Herbs de Provence or oregano
1 tsp paprika
1 tbsp Dijon mustard
Fresh herbs such as parsley, cilantro, chopped (optional)
1 pound meat (ground beef, sausage, a mix of both)
1 cup white rice
½ cup water or broth (see recipe p.209)

Cut the tops off the tomatoes. Hollow out the insides of the tomatoes with a knife. Set aside pulp and juice. Salt the inside of the tomatoes and put them upside down on an absorbent paper towel. In a bowl, prepare the stuffing mixing together onion, garlic, bread, spices, and meat. Preheat the oven to 400° F. Pour a drizzle of oil in the bottom of your dish. Spread the rice. Optionally, add a little tomato pulp and mix with the rice. Stuff the tomatoes one by one, cover with the caps and arrange them on the rice. Heat broth or water in the microwave. Pour over the rice. Drizzle the tops of the stuffed tomatoes with a drizzle of olive oil. Bake for 45 minutes. If after 30 minutes, the rice has absorbed all the water and is not yet cooked, add about ¼ cup hot water.

Soups and Stews

> "Soup is a comforting dish, easily concocted, easily digested and universally acceptable."
>
> -Helen Nearing, American author, advocate of simple living

I love soups! They are the most forgiving meals. They are so versatile. They can be smooth and creamy, thin and clear, full of vegetables, or thickened with rice and pasta. You can't really fail soups. They can be made out of almost anything and almost out of nothing. You don't need elaborate cooking skills to make them. They are often very cheap and can feed a big crowd in no time. They also have the advantage of being made in advance. They are easy to reheat and they freeze well. In a nutshell, soups check all the criteria for simplicity and nourishment. There is no more wholesome, nutritious, and economic food than soups. Add a delicious slice of fresh homemade bread and call it a meal!

There are different types of soups:
- A **stew** is a combination of solid food ingredients that have been cooked in water or other water-based liquid, typically by simmering, and are then served without being drained.
- A **soup** is very similar to a stew. It will generally have more liquid. There are two categories of soups: clear soup and thick soup. Clear soups include bouillon, broth, and consommé. Thick soups include velouté, cream, and pureed soups.

Some tips to make delicious soups:
- With the right blend of spices, you can bring a simmering pot of vegetables cooked in broth to the next level, giving it an international flair: Asian, Thai, Moroccan, Mexican, and more.
- Condiments are key: slivered almonds, fresh herbs, fermented golden raisins, preserved lemons, cream, cheese....
- Kitchen sink soup: Have you ever looked in the refrigerator and found you have half of a bell pepper, half squash, a quarter of an onion, etc. Vegetable soup is the perfect plan to use up all of those odds and ends.

Vegetarian Chili Tortilla Soup (Instant Pot®)

This vegetarian tortilla soup is a staple at our house. A really easy recipe, using just one pot and that doesn't need a lot of prep work. The perfect make-ahead dish for easy lunches and dinners. Top it with avocado, cilantro, or tortilla chips for a comforting meal. And the best part? Leftovers are even better the next day. I made this vegetarian tortilla soup in my Instant Pot® but you can easily make it on a stove-top too.

Olive oil or ghee
1 onion, chopped
4 garlic cloves, minced
1 red bell pepper, chopped
One 14 oz can black beans, drained and rinsed
One 14 oz can pinto beans, drained and rinsed
One 14 oz can dice tomato (or tomato sauce)
1 cup red lentils
1 tsp chili powder
1 tsp garlic powder
1 tsp cumin
¼ tsp cayenne pepper
3 cups vegetable, chicken, or beef broth (see recipe p.209)
Salt or homemade bouillon paste, to taste (see recipe p.207)
1 cup corn (I use frozen corn)

Press the sauté button on the Instant Pot®. Add some olive oil or ghee to the pot and then add onion, garlic, bell pepper. Sauté for 3 to 4 minutes until the onions are softened. Add in the drained and rinsed black beans and pinto beans, diced tomatoes, and red lentils. Add the spices and the broth. Stir to combine. Close the pot with its lid. Press the manual or pressure cook button and cook on high pressure for 10 minutes, with the pressure valve in the sealing position. Let the pressure release naturally. Open the lid and add the frozen corn. Mix to combine. Ladle vegetarian tortilla soup into individual bowls, and top with your favorite toppings: tortilla chips, diced avocado, jalapenos, cilantro, or lime wedges.

Ramen Noodle Soup (Instant Pot®)

I remember my Wednesday lunch as a middle schooler. As soon as I got home, I hurried to cook some ground beef steak with two packages of instant noodles. I devoured it in a couple of minutes. I guess this recipe is a better-for-you, more grown-up version of your childhood / college days favorite.

1 ½ cup chicken or vegetable broth (see recipe p.209)
2 tsp soy sauce
1 tsp sesame oil (for stovetop method)
1 tsp dried minced onion (or onion powder)
1 tsp garlic powder
½ tsp ground ginger
1 block of ramen noodle
1 small carrot, thinly sliced
1 cup thinly shredded vegetables such as Napa cabbage, spinach, kale, or other greens
A few button, cremini, or shiitake mushrooms, thinly sliced
Chopped green onion, for garnish

Pour the broth in the Instant Pot® and add all the spices. Add the ramen noodles, shredded carrots, vegetables, and mushrooms. Place the lid on your Instant Pot® and turn the valve to sealing. Set the cook time to 1 minute on high pressure. When cooking time is complete, turn the valve to do a quick release. Carefully remove the lid and with a fork loosen the noodles and mix them together with the broth. Pour the noodles and the broth into a bowl and serve hot. Top with green onions.

Stovetop Method:

In a medium saucepan, combine broth, spices, mushrooms, and noodles. Cover and bring to a boil over high heat. Stir to break up noodles. Simmer, uncovered, for 10 minutes. Stir in sesame oil and garnish with green onions.

Soupe des chevaliers (Knight soup) (Instant Pot®)

The name of this soup came out one night at the dinner table. I was serving a stew with potatoes, carrots, onions, lentils, and meat. And my husband started saying that it could have been the kind of soup they served during Middle Age times... Hence Knight Soup. When my daughters were toddlers, they enjoyed eating dishes with interesting names. I just love the flavor of that soup. A very comforting winter stew.

> *Oil, butter or ghee for the pot*
> *1 onion, diced*
> *4 garlic cloves, peeled and finely chopped*
> *1 pound meat (pork shoulder, chicken, or beef)*
> *6 medium carrots, peeled and chopped*
> *4 potatoes, peeled and diced*
> *1 cup brown lentils*
> *1 bay leaf*
> *4 cups broth (see recipe p.209)*
> *Salt or 1 tbsp homemade Better Than Bouillon Paste (see recipe p. 207)*

Set the Instant Pot® to sauté and heat the oil. Add onion, garlic, and meat and cook for a few seconds. Add carrots, potatoes, lentils, bay leaf, and broth. Seal the pot and cook for 10mn on high pressure.

Carrot Soup

I always have carrots at the bottom of my fridge. This soup is my go-to soup recipe during wintertime. My daughters named it "The orange soup." For a naturally sweeter version, sauté onions over low heat for 20 minutes.

> *Olive oil or butter for the pot*
> *1 onion, diced*
> *7 medium size carrots, cut into 1-inch pieces (about 2 ½ cups)*
> *1 medium sweet potato, peeled and diced*
> *1 tsp cumin*
> *1 tbsp fresh ginger (optional)*
> *3 cups chicken or vegetable broth (see recipe p.209)*
> *1 tsp salt or homemade bouillon paste (see recipe p.207)*

Heat some olive oil or butter in a heavy-bottomed saucepan over medium heat. Add onions, carrots, sweet potato, cumin, and ginger. Sauté for 1 minute. Add broth and salt (or homemade better than bouillon). Bring the mixture to a boil, then turn down the heat and simmer gently for 20 minutes. For a velouté texture, transfer the soup in a high-powered blender such as a Vitamix. Otherwise, use an immersion blender.

For the Instant Pot® version:
Set the Instant Pot® to sauté and heat the oil. Add onion, carrots, sweet potato, cumin, and ginger. Mix well and sauté for 1 minute. Add broth and salt. Seal the pot and cook for 1 minute on high pressure.

Leek Potato Parsnip Cauliflower Soup (Instant Pot®)

This soup is a concentrate of not so loved vegetables here in the U.S. So many times, I had to tell the cashier at the grocery store the name of this long white and green vegetable...

¼ cup olive oil

3 leeks, rinsed of grit and finely chopped*

1 small celery root, diced

2 parsnips, diced

1 cup cauliflower, diced

1 large potato, peeled and diced

½ tsp sea salt or homemade bouillon paste, to taste (see recipe p.207)

1 tsp pepper

½ tsp dried thyme

1 bay leaf

6 to 8 cups vegetable broth (see recipe p.209)

Set your Instant Pot® to sauté and heat the oil. Add leeks, celery root, parsnips, and cauliflower and cook for about 5 minutes. Then add potato, salt, pepper, thyme, bay leaf, and 6 to 8 cups of broth and cook on high pressure for 12 minutes, then release pressure with a manual release.

*Leeks are notorious for having bits of sand and dirt lodged throughout. I like to chop them before cleaning. Then I cover them with cold water in a bowl and swish them around with my hands to dislodge the dirt. Change the water and repeat if necessary. Drain in a colander.

Tomato Pesto Cauliflower Soup (Instant Pot®)

I discovered this recipe in the book The Plant Paradox Family Cookbook by Steven Gundry. I was curious about the fact that this tomato soup recipe called for cauliflower. The soup tastes really good. My daughters even asked for second helping. Delicious with a good homemade slice of bread.

Oil or butter for the pot

1 onion

1 pound cauliflower florets

1 tsp salt or homemade bouillon paste (see recipe p.207)

1 tsp garlic powder

1 tsp dried oregano

1 tsp paprika

1 tsp dried basil

Two 28 ounces cans diced tomatoes

One 14.5 oz can cannellini beans (white beans)

4 cups vegetable broth (see recipe p.209)

1 tbsp lemon juice

¼ cup basil pesto

Set the Instant Pot® to sauté and heat the oil. Add the onion, cauliflower, salt, garlic powder, oregano, paprika, and basil. Stir occasionally until the onion is wilted. Add tomatoes, cannellini beans, broth, lemon juice, and pesto and seal the pot. Cook for 15 minutes on high pressure. Blend the soup with an immersion blender, until creamy.

Moroccan Stew

The spices of this stew will bring you comfort in times of challenging days. My dear friend, Tania, offered my family this delicious meal with some veal, and couscous on the side, when we had a meal train (when friends and family pitch in and cook meals for one in need) after the birth of our fourth daughter. I will always remember this dish! Since then, I tweaked the recipe to make it in my Instant Pot® to save me some time. But you can easily make it on the stove.

2 tbsp olive oil, butter or ghee

1 onion, chopped

2 cups butternut squash or sweet potatoes, peeled and diced

Two 14 ounce can chickpeas (without the liquid and rinsed)

One 28 ounce can diced tomatoes

One 14 ounce can coconut milk

1 tbsp Moroccan spice mix (see recipe page 205)

3 garlic cloves

Salt or homemade bouillon paste (see recipe p.210)

Set the Instant Pot® to sauté and heat the oil. Add onion, garlic, butternut squash/sweet potato, and spices. Sauté for a few minutes. Add coconut milk, chickpeas, and tomatoes and seal the pot. Cook for 10 minutes on high pressure.

Date Red Lentils Stew

This stew is a hit in our home, especially for my vegetarian daughter, Coline. It is one of the only stews she is ok to bring in for lunch at school. That says a lot! The final touch of chopped dates adds some much sweetness to this stew. Very warming with tons of great spices. A perfect stew for a chilly day. Don't be intimidated by the long list of ingredients! They are mostly spices.

1 tsp ground paprika

1 tsp ground turmeric

1 tsp ground ginger

1 tsp ground coriander

½ tsp ground nutmeg

⅛ tsp ground cloves

olive oil (or butter or ghee- see recipe p.212)

1 onion, finely chopped

3 garlic cloves

4 celery stalks, chopped

3 medium size carrots, chopped

4 ripe tomatoes or one 14oz can diced tomatoes

3 cups cooked chickpeas (or two 14oz cans of garbanzo beans)

1 cup red lentils

5 cups broth (see recipe p.209)

2 tsp salt or homemade bouillon paste, to taste (see recipe p.210)
1 cinnamon stick
½ cup dates, finely chopped
Parsley, cilantro, slivered almonds, cheese for garnish

In a small bowl, combine all the ground spices together. In a large pot, heat some olive oil (butter or ghee) on medium heat and add the chopped onion. Cook until tender. Add chopped garlic and the spices. Mix thoroughly. Add chopped celery and carrots. Mix well and cook for about 2 minutes. Then add tomatoes, chickpeas, and red lentils. Mix well. Add broth and cinnamon stick. Cook for about 20 minutes. Add the dates and mix well. When you are ready to serve, top the stew with slivered almonds, parsley, and cilantro.

Note: This recipe is very easy to make with the Instant Pot®. Follow the same directions. Start using the function Sauté and then, once everything is in the pot, cook on high pressure for 10 minutes. Once it is ready, turn the venting knob from the sealing position to the venting position. (Make sure the steam has stopped flowing and the floating valve has dropped before opening the lid). Add the dates.

Sweets and Snacks

In France, there is a national consensus around snack time. It is usually around 4 p.m. We call it "le goûter" or the 4 o'clock. Most of the time it is a sweet collation. When I was a kid, the most traditional and favorite snack was a piece of baguette with some butter and a chocolate bar in the middle, or some easy and simple homemade cakes (hello, yogurt cake). When we moved to the U.S, I discovered a whole new meaning to snacks. Snacking is often the way to eat meals here. After more than 10 years of living in the U.S., we haven't changed our regular mealtimes: breakfast, lunch, 4 o'clock snack, and dinner. Having regular mealtimes really helps regulate your energy throughout the day.

French also like to end their meals on a sweet note: A good piece of dark chocolate to go with a coffee, a yogurt, fruit, a pastry, or a slice of pie.

*****

Some Interesting Facts About Sugar

"Sugar is the tobacco of the 21st century
and probably the most dangerous part of our current diet."
– Mark Bittman

For reference, 1 teaspoon sugar = 4g sugar.

Recommendation for daily added sugar intake from the World Health Organization (WHO) and American Heart Association (AHA):

- 6 teaspoons (25 grams) for women
- 9 teaspoons (38 grams) for men
- 3-6 teaspoons (12 - 25 grams) for children

The average American consumes 17 teaspoons (71.14 grams) every day. That translates into about 57 pounds of added sugar consumed each year, per person. Sugar is not used in a traditional way anymore and is hidden everywhere, making it very challenging to realize the daily amount consumed.

There are more than 60 different names for sugar (like dextrose, sucrose, maltose, high fructose corn syrup, dextrin, malt syrup, juice concentrate, barley malt, agave nectar, beet sugar, fructose, glucose, honey, turbinado, sorghum syrup...).

****

Here are Some Tips to Reduce Your Intake of Sugar

Avoid the following foods as much as possible:

- **Soft drinks**: Whether you call it soda or pop, soft drinks alone often contain your total daily intake of added sugar.
- **Fruit juices**: Did you know fruit juices can have as much sugar as soft drinks? Make your own smoothies instead!
- **Candies** & **Sweets**: Candies and sweets obviously offer no nutritional value.
- **Baked goods**: Cookies, cakes, and pies are usually high in sugar and refined carbohydrates that make you crave them even more.
- **Fruits canned in syrup**: Eat whole fruits and vegetables instead.
- **Food labeled "Low-fat"**: This type of food makes up the loss of fat with higher amounts of added sugar.

I think the best way to have more control around our sugar intake is to bake our own treats with natural and the least refined sources of sugar (fruit, coconut sugar, honey, or maple syrup). That way, you control the amount and quality. I have noticed that usually when I follow a recipe found on the internet, I reduce the sugar amount by half. I also like to use fruits to sweeten a cake (apples, applesauce, bananas, and dates work great).

Yogurt Cake

This is THE cake of my childhood. It is probably the first cake a French kid learns to bake, using a yogurt pot as a measurement. This format of yogurt is not that prevalent in the U.S. but once you figure out that one pot equals half a cup, you are good to go! For some reason, during our first years in the U.S., I failed this cake many times. It was rising well in the oven and then a big flop appeared. Plus, the texture was rubbery. Once I figured out that I am not supposed to use Greek Yogurt for that recipe, I was able to recreate the cake from my childhood. This cake still remains the one I am craving for snacks. If I am totally transparent with you, I often make it just to enjoy licking the bowl with the raw batter.

¾ cup sugar
Zest of one lemon or an orange (optional)
3 eggs
1 cup plain whole milk yogurt
½ cup olive oil
1 ½ cup all-purpose flour or cake flour (see recipe p.226)
1 tbsp baking powder (see recipe p.225)
½ tsp salt

Preheat the oven at 350° F and grease a pan. In a bowl, mix sugar, and zests (if you use them). Add eggs, yogurt, and olive oil. Combine well. Gradually add flour, baking powder, and salt.

Pour the batter in a greased pan and bake in the oven for 55 minutes. Let it cool down for 20 minutes.

Chocolate Marble Yogurt Cake Variation

Omit the citrus zest and replace with some vanilla extract. Scoop ⅓ of the cake batter into a small bowl and gently stir in 3 tablespoons of cocoa powder until well-mixed. Alternate one spoon of chocolate batter with one spoon of vanilla batter when pouring in the cake pan. You can also add chocolate chips or pieces of fruit (apples, blueberries...).

Chocolate Cake

>   *7oz dark chocolate, broken down into small pieces*
>   *3 eggs*
>   *½ cup sugar*
>   *1 tsp vanilla extract*
>   *⅔ cup applesauce*
>   *½ cup cornstarch, all-purpose flour or almond flour*
>   *2 tsp baking powder (see recipe p.225)*
>   *Pinch of salt*

Preheat the oven to 350° F. Melt chocolate using a microwave or a double boiler. In a bowl, mix eggs, sugar, and vanilla extract. Add melted chocolate and applesauce. Mix well. Add flour, baking powder and salt. Mix until you have a smooth batter. Transfer in greased baking 8x8 pan and bake for 25 minutes.

Water Cakes: Lemon and Chocolate Versions

As I am writing this book, the price of food is going up, up, and up. I can't help but think about my grandparents who survived World War II and for some of them World War I, when food scarcity was a real deal. Baking with water, with no egg and dairy? Why not? These two cakes are extremely moist and very easy to put together and you already probably have all the ingredients in your pantry.

Lemon Cake

1 ½ cup all-purpose flour or cake flour (see recipe p.226))

½ to ¾ cup sugar cup sugar

1 ½ tsp baking powder (see recipe p.225)

Zest of one lemon

4 tsp lemon juice

¼ cup olive oil

1 cup lukewarm water

½ tsp almond extract (optional)

Chocolate Cake

1 ½ cup all-purpose flour

4 tbsp cocoa powder

1 tsp baking powder (see recipe p.225)

1 tsp baking soda

½ tsp salt

½ to ¾ cup sugar

1 tsp vanilla extract

1 tbsp vinegar

5 tbsp oil

1 cup lukewarm water

Preheat the oven at 325° F and grease an 8x8 pan. In a bowl, combine the dry ingredients. Add wet ingredients to the bowl and mix well. Pour the mixture in a greased pan and bake for 45 to 50 minutes. Let it cool down.

Fruit Clafoutis

I love this recipe. It is a staple dessert in France. Very easy to make, versatile, and at the same time so elegant. You can use individual ramekins, a tart mold, or a regular baking dish to bake it. Delicious right out of the oven or cooler. A scoop of vanilla ice cream is often a great addition to this dessert.

2 cups fruit (apples, pears, cherries, strawberries, apricots, peaches...), chopped*
1 cup all-purpose flour
½ cup sugar
3 eggs
3 tbsp melted butter
1 ⅓ cup cow milk or almond milk
1 tsp vanilla extract
1 tsp of rum (optional)

Preheat the oven at 375° F. Grease a rectangular pan and fill it with chopped fruits (or a combination of fruits). In a bowl, mix flour, sugar, eggs, butter, and add the milk. Add vanilla extract and rum. Pour the batter over the fruits and bake in the oven for 40 minutes or until golden.

*Use enough fruit to fill out the bottom of the pan.

Apple Tart

This is the first pie I learned to bake when I was a kid. I love this recipe as it is not too sweet. The filling and topping are naturally sweetened with applesauce and sliced apples. Simple and delicious.

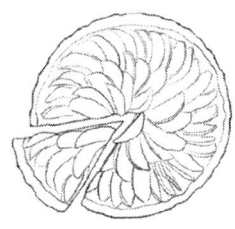

One sweet pie crust (see recipe p.238)
1 to 2 cups homemade or store-bought applesauce
2 apples, peeled and finely sliced
For the glaze: 2 tbsp apricot jam with 1 tbsp water (optional)

Preheat the oven at 375° F. Parbake the crust for 10mn. Get the pie crust out of the oven. Cover the crust with applesauce. Starting from the outside, arrange the apple slices in a spiral pattern, overlapping one another until the entire surface is covered. Bake the pie until the apple slices start turning brown. Remove the pie from the oven… To make the glaze, heat the apricot jam and water in a small pan, and strain into a bowl. Remove the tart from the oven and, while still warm, use a pastry brush to coast the apple with the warm glaze. Serve either warm or at room temperature plain, with crème fraîche or vanilla ice cream.

Lemon Tart

This tart is among the first ones I tried when I was dating my husband. I found it on the popular French website, Marmiton.fr. Since then, I have been making it very regularly. It is easy and what still amazes me is that this recipe doesn't require butter and yet the result is amazing: lemony and creamy. A must-try if you are a fan of lemon flavor.

One sweet pie crust (see recipe p.238)
2 lemons, juiced and zested
2 eggs, beaten
⅓ cup sugar
1 tbsp cornstarch
1 pinch salt

Preheat oven to 370° F. Blind-bake the pie crust using parchment paper and dried beans on top. In a medium saucepan, heat lemon zest, juice, sugar, cornstarch, and salt over medium heat until sugar is dissolved. Pour egg mixture into the pan and whisk to prevent curdling. Whisk, until mixture has thickened, about 5 minutes. Pour the lemon curd over the pie crust.

No-Bake Strawberry Pie

This is my most favorite spring treat when strawberries are in season. When we lived in Durham, NC, we had this tradition to go strawberry picking in April. It was such a wonderful experience for the family. As soon as we came back home, I rushed to my tiny kitchen to prepare this dessert. Moving to Sioux Falls, SD, I added a little twist to the recipe with the addition of some vanilla custard. I like to use the silicone muffin tins to make individual tartlets. But you can also use a regular 9-inch pie dish. The service will be a little more challenging as the pie crust is crumbly.

One no-bake pie crust (see recipe p.238)
1 vanilla custard (see separate recipe p.226)
1 strawberry custard
10 strawberries, rinsed and sliced
1 tbsp lemon juice
1 tbsp sugar

In a bowl, marinate the sliced strawberries with lemon juice and sugar. Set aside. Make the no-bake pie crust. Pour it at the bottom of a pan, or in individual silicone muffin molds. Set it in the fridge while you prepare the custards. Make the vanilla custard. Make the strawberry custard. Assemble the pie: Pour the strawberry custard on the pie crust. Cover with the vanilla custard. Top it with the strawberries.

Strawberry Custard

1-pound fresh strawberries, rinsed and roughly chopped
½ cup water
¼ cup sugar

¼ cup cornstarch

Put all the ingredients in a saucepan. With a hand mixer, purée the mixture. Cook over medium heat. Use a spatula or a whisker and keep mixing until it thickens (about 5 minutes). Pour the custard on the pie crust.

Gluten-Free Chocolate cookies

I love this very easy recipe. No egg, no dairy necessary. You can make a batch in no time when you crave something sweet. Makes about 12 cookies.

1 ½ cup almond flour
½ tsp baking powder (see recipe p.225)
3 tbsp coconut oil or olive oil
3 tbsp maple syrup
1 tsp vanilla extract
1 tsp salt
¼ cup chocolate chips

Preheat the oven to 350° F. Use a baking sheet and cover it with parchment paper. In a bowl, mix all the ingredients together. Place 12 scoops of batter on the sheet and flatten them with the palm of your hands. Bake for about 10mn or until the bottom of the cookies is brown. Let the cookies cool down before transferring them

Bliss Balls

If you're not a fan of baking, you can still whip up an indulgent snack without taking too much time. Nut Balls, Date Balls, Bliss Balls, and Energy Bites are here to meet your needs. These pick-me-ups are a simple concoction of whole, raw ingredients blended together and then rolled into a convenient ball that you can bring anywhere and eat any time! It can be as simple as a blend of two ingredients (nuts + dates –

Nature's candy) or a more elaborate creation with the addition of spices, seeds, oats, and nut butter. You choose!

When it comes to making energy balls, you want to keep in mind a few rules to make them work. You'll need a combination of ingredients that are:
- Sticky (usually dried fruit)
- Crunchy (usually nuts & seeds)
- Creamy (usually nut butter or coconut oil)

The formula below is for the most standard energy ball, with no flavors or extras added in. I'll give you some pointers after for customizing.
- *1 cup Medjool dates*
- *1 cup nuts and seeds*
- *2 – 3 tbsp nut butter*

You just blend that up in a food processor, roll them into balls and you're good to go!

There is no end to the possibilities with the flavor you want to give
- Dried Fruit: dates, figs, raisins, dried apples/mangoes, dried berries
- Nuts/Seeds: use any combination you'd like – almonds, pecans, walnuts, hazelnuts, pumpkin seeds, sunflower seeds, chia seeds
- Flavored Powders: adding things like cacao powder, protein powder, maca is a great way to change up the flavor
- Spices: cinnamon, nutmeg, turmeric, vanilla, and pumpkin pie spice

Note: This recipe can be used as a crust for no bake tarts.

Multi-purpose 4-Ingredient Caramel Sauce

This is the simplest recipe to create the silkiest and creamiest caramel sauce. All it takes is 4 ingredients and 5 minutes of your time. This sauce is the perfect addition to drizzle over pancakes, waffles, cakes, yogurts, fresh fruits, or ice cream. You name it!

> ¼ cup maple syrup
>
> ¼ cup tahini
>
> 2 tbsp coconut oil
>
> ½ tsp salt

In a small saucepan, heat maple syrup, tahini, and coconut oil over low heat. Add salt and stir until well combined. Transfer the caramel into a container. Store in the refrigerator for up to two weeks.

Note: The consistency of the caramel depends on the thickness of the tahini. The thicker the tahini paste, the thicker the caramel sauce.

Roasted Chickpeas

This recipe requires only 5 minutes of active prep time with just a few ingredients. You can customize it to your personal taste by adding spices (cumin, chipotle, chili powder...) or simply some sea salt.

> One 15-ounce can chickpeas, rinsed and dry
>
> 1 tbsp olive oil
>
> ½ tsp salt
>
> 1 tsp spices of your choice (paprika, cumin, coriander...)

Preheat the oven to 400° F. Rinse the canned chickpeas using a strainer. Use a towel to rub the chickpeas in a circular motion, discarding any skins that fall off. Place the chickpeas on a baking sheet and let them get dry to the touch. It is important that they are dry before coating them in oil or they will not get crunchy when roasted. Alternatively, you can place the baking sheet with the chickpeas in the oven while it preheats, evaporating the remaining moisture. Coat the chickpeas with oil and the seasoning of your choice. Roast for 40 minutes, shaking in a circular motion every 15 minutes to ensure even roasting. Set the tray on a cooling rack. Chickpeas can be stored in an airtight container for 5 to 7 days.

Get to Know Sandrine with Her Favorite Quotes and Mantras That Guide Her Life

Lifestyle

Simplify to amplify.

We are spiritual beings having a human experience.

"Beliefs are the hidden scripts that run our lives. They underpin every action we take and how we interpret and respond to the world around us."
-Marie Forleo, thought leader, American entrepreneur

"Every action you take is a vote for the type of person you want to become."
-James Clear, author of *Atomic Habits*

"Very little is needed to make a happy life; it is all within yourself, in your way of thinking."
-Marcus Aurelius, Stoic philosopher

JOMO (Joy Of Missing Out) vs FOMO (Fear Of Missing Out). JOMO is an intense feeling of delight and happiness caused by centering your life on what is truly important and letting go of the 'Shoulds" and "Have Tos" in life.

"I've learned that people will forget what you said, people will forget what you did but people will never forget the way you made them feel."
-Maya Angelou, American memoirist, poet, and civil rights activist

"Life is a dance between making it happen and letting it happen."
-Arianna Huffington, Greek-American author

"We don't stop playing because we grow old; we grow old because we stop playing."

-George Bernard Shaw, Irish playwright, critic, political activist

"The need for connection and community is primal, as fundamental as the need for air, water, and food."
-Dean Ornish, American physician and researcher

"In a world where we are able to jump on an app to order dinner, get a ride from a stranger, or even pay our bills, there seems to be a decreasing need for human interactions. Technology is a tool that has allowed countless advances in medicine, psychology, industry, and more, but it's also allowing us to automate ourselves away from human connection and personal intimacy - creating more emotionally detached people than ever before in history."
-Lisa Strohma, psychologist and founder of Digital Citizen Academy

"Technology is a useful servant but a dangerous master."
-Christian Lous Lange, Norwegian historian, teacher, and political scientist, winner of the Nobel Peace Prize in 1921

Health

"Self-care is the real health care."
-Randi Kay, holistic health practitioner and educator

If you don't listen to your body whisper, then you will hear it scream.

Most pain was created through small and steady habits, and they heal through small and steady habits.

Parenting

Kahlil Gibran Poem "On children."
-The prophet

Your children are not your children.
They are the sons and daughters of Life's longing for itself.
They come through you but not from you,
And though they are with you yet they belong not to you.
You may give them your love but not your thoughts,
For they have their own thoughts.
You may house their bodies but not their souls,
For their souls dwell in the house of tomorrow, which you cannot visit, not even in your dreams.
You may strive to be like them, but seek not to make them like you.
For life goes not backward nor tarries with yesterday.
You are the bows from which your children as living arrows are sent forth.
The archer sees the mark upon the path of the infinite, and He bends you with His might that His arrows may go swift and far.
Let your bending in the archer's hand be for gladness;
For even as He loves the arrow that flies, so He loves also the bow that is stable.
The best gift you can give to your children is your own happiness.

"Your children need your presence more than your presents."
-Jesse Jackson, American political activist

"People without children thought that having a newborn was the hardest part of parenthood, that upside-down, day-is-night twilight zone of feedings and toothless wails. But parents knew better. Parents knew that the hardest part of parenthood was figuring out how to do the right thing twenty-four hours a day, forever, and surviving all the times you failed."
-Emma Straub, American novelist, author of *All Adults Here*

Connection with Nature

"In the indigenous view, humans are viewed as somewhat lesser beings in the democracy of species. We are referred to as the younger brothers of Creation, so like younger brothers we must learn from our elders. Plants were here first and have had a long time to figure things out. They live both adobe and below ground and hold the earth in place. Plants know how to make food from light and water. Not only do they feed themselves, but they make enough to sustain the lives of all the rest of us. Plants are providers for the rest of the community and exemplify the virtue of generosity, always offering food."
-Robin Wall Kimmerer, American Distinguished Teaching Professor of Environmental and Forest Biology; and Director, Center for Native Peoples and the Environment

"I understood at a very early age that in Nature, I felt everything I should feel in church but never did. Walking in the woods, I felt in touch with the universe and with the spirit of the universe."
-Alice Walker, American novelist, poet, social activist

Additional Reading and Resources: Books, Food Blogs, Websites, & Podcasts

American Women Who Experienced the French Way of Living

Bard, Elizabeth. (2011). *Lunch in Paris: A Love Story, with Recipes.* Back Bay Books.

Druckerman, Pamela. (2014). *Bringing Up Bébé: One American Mother Discovers the Wisdom of French Parenting.* Penguin Books.

Herrmann Loomis, Suzanne. (2016). *In a French Kitchen: Tales and Traditions of Everyday Home Cooking in France.* Avery.

LeBillon, Karen. (2014). *French Kids Eat Everything: How Our Family Moved to France, Cured Picky Eating, Banned Snacking, and Discovered 10 Simple Rules for Raising Happy, Healthy Eaters.* William Morrow Paperbacks.

Mah, Ann. (2014). *Mastering the Art of French Eating: From Paris Bistros to Farmhouse Kitchens, Lessons in Food and Love.* Penguin Books.

Marshall, Jeannie. (2014). *The Lost Art of Feeding Kids: What Italy Taught Me about Why Children Need Real Food.* Beacon Press.

Waters, Alice. (2007). *The Art of Simple Food: Notes, Lessons, and Recipes from a Delicious Revolution: A Cookbook.* Clarkson Potter.

Food Blogger, Beeta with Mon Petit Four

French Women Who ShareTheir Love for French Food

Barrial, Aurélie. (2019). *Cooking for $1.* Independently published.

Delarue, Cécile. (2015). *The Everything Easy French Cookbook: Includes Boeuf Bourguignon, Crepes Suzette, Croque-Monsieur Maison, Quiche Lorraine, Mousse au Chocolat...and Hundreds More!* Everything; Illustrated edition.

Delarue, Cécile. (2017). *Voilà! The Effortless French Cookbook: Easy Recipes to Savor the Classic Tastes of France.* Rockridge Press.

Guiliano, Mireille. (2007). *French Women Don't Get Fat: The Secret of Eating for Pleasure*. Vintage; Reprint edition.

Peltre Béatrice. (2012). *La Tartine Gourmande: Recipes for an Inspired Life*. Roost Books.

Peltre Béatrice. (2016). *My French Family Table: Recipes for a Life Filled with Food, Love, and Joie de Vivre*. Roost Books.

Tracy, Estelle. (2016). *Guide de survie alimentaire aux Etats-Unis (French Edition)*. Independently published.

Food Blogger, Clotilde Dusoulier with Chocolate & Zucchini

Food Blogger, Catherine Katz with Cuisinicity

Food Blogger, Delphine Fortin with Del's Cooking Twist

Food Blogger, Béatrice Peltre with Tartine Gourmande

Books About Wellness and Self-Development

Clear, James. (2018). *Atomic Habits: An Easy & Proven Way to Build Good Habits & Break Bad Ones*. Avery; Illustrated edition.

Duhigg, Charles. (2014). *The Power of Habit: Why We Do What We Do in Life and Business*

Forleo, Marie. (2019). *Everything Is Figureoutable*. Portfolio; First edition.

Nestor James. (2020). *Breath: The New Science of a Lost Art*. Riverhead Books.

Northrup, Kate. (2019). *Do Less: A Revolutionary Approach to Time and Energy Management for Ambitious Women*. Hay House Inc.

Strickler, Yancey. (2019). *This Could Be Our Future: A Manifesto for a More Generous World*. Viking; 1st Edition.

Stroke, Amy. (2014). *Homemade Beauty: 150 Simple Beauty Recipes Made from All-Natural Ingredients*. TarcherPerigee; Illustrated edition.

Wright, Glenn Amy. (2013). *Birth, Breath, and Death: Meditations on Motherhood, Chaplaincy, and Life as a Doula*. Independently published.

Resources About Healthy Eating

Bittman, Mark, & Katz, David. (2020). *How To Eat: All Your Food and Diet Questions Answered.* Harvest; 1st edition.

Hale Sofia Schatz. (2004). *If the Buddha Came to Dinner: How to Nourish Your Body to Awaken Your Spirit.* Hachette Books; Illustrated edition.

Hari Vani, *Feeding You Lies: How to Unravel the Food Industry's Playbook and Reclaim Your Health.* Hay House Inc.

Nestle, Marion. (2018). *Unsavory Truth: How Food Companies Skew the Science of What We Eat.* Basic Books; 1st edition.

Jacobsen, Maryann. (2019). *The Family Dinner Solution: How to Create a Rotation of Dinner Meals Your Family Will Love.* RMI Books; 2nd edition.

Nearing, Helen. (1990). *Simple Food for the Good Life: Random Acts of Cooking and Pithy Quotations (Good Life Series).* Chelsea Green Publishing.

Panda, Satchin. (2018). *The Circadian Code: Lose Weight, Supercharge Your Energy, and Transform Your Health from Morning to Midnight.* Rodale Books; Illustrated edition.

Pollan, Michael. (2011). *Food Rules: An Eater's Manual.* Penguin Press; Illustrated edition.

Pollan, Michael. (2008). *In Defense of Food: An Eater's Manifesto.* Penguin Press; 1st edition.

Wolever, Ruth, & Reardon, Beth, with Hannan Tania. (2016). *The Mindful Diet: How to Transform Your Relationship with Food for Lasting Weight Loss and Vibrant Health.* Scribener.

Resources About Slow Food / Real Food Movement

Fallon, Sally. (1995). *Nourishing Traditions: The Cookbook that Challenges Politically Correct Nutrition and Diet Dictocrats.* Newtrends Publishing, Inc.; 2nd Revised edition

Kingsolver, Barbara. (2008). *Animal, Vegetable, Miracle: A Year of Food Life.* Harper Perennial; Reprint edition.

Planck, Nina. (2016). *Real Food: What to Eat and Why.* Bloomsbury USA; Reprint edition.

Prentice, Jessica. (2006). *Full Moon Feast: Food and the Hunger for Connection.* Chelsea Green Publishing.

Waters, Alice. (2017). *Coming to My Senses: The Making of a Counterculture Cook.* Clarkson Potter; Illustrated edition.

Waters, Alice. (2021) *We Are What We Eat: A Slow Food Manifesto.* Penguin Press.

Resources About Feeding Families

Adachi, Kendra. (2022). *The Lazy Genius Kitchen: Have What You Need, Use What You Have, Enjoy It Like Never Before.* WaterBrook Edition

Maryann Jacobsen's books found on her website.

Satter, Ellyn. (2000). *Child of Mine: Feeding with Love and Good Sense, Revised and Updated Edition.* Bull Publishing Company; Revised edition.

Satter, Ellyn. (2008). *Secrets of Feeding a Healthy Family: How to Eat, How to Raise Good Eaters, How to Cook.* Kelcy Press; 2nd edition.

The Family Dinner Project

My Favorite Food Blogs
Where I Find Great Inspiration and Meal Ideas

100 Days of Real Food by Lisa Leake

Detoxinista by Megan Gilmore

Pinch Of Yum by Lindsay Ostrom

Smitten Kitchen by Deb Perelman

This Pilgrim Life by Lisa Burns

The amazing team behind Minimalist Baker

My Favorite Podcasts to Listen to When I Cook

Adachi, Kendra. (Host). *The Lazy Genius* [Audio podcast].

Barahona, Denaye. (Host). *Simple Families the Podcast* [Audio podcast].

Doyle, Glennon. (Host). *We Can Do Hard Things* [Audio podcast].

Kay, Randi. (Host). *Simple Self Care Podcast* [Audio podcast].

Webster, Riley. (Host). *The Kismet Collection* [Audio podcast].

About the Author

Sandrine Pilaz is a French woman who wears many hats: mother, wife, daughter, sister, friend, health coach, animal and nature lover. Born and raised in France, she has been living in the U.S. for more than a decade. She started her American expatriation in Baltimore, Maryland and Durham, North Carolina. She currently lives in the Midwest, in Sioux Falls, South Dakota with her husband and four daughters, their dog Mako, and cat Sansa. Her life is all about finding beauty in its simple pleasures. She believes that simplicity is the essence of happiness. She loves tent camping, hiking, traveling, dancing, cooking, and connecting with people and nature, away from technology. She also identifies herself in a more global way as a citizen of this world, a connector, a seeker, and a life-long learner. You can learn more about Sandrine on her personal French blog, 6OutWest.com, and on her website, www.sandrinepilaz.com. This is her first book.

Made in the USA
Columbia, SC
31 October 2022